The *Lamp*

Psalm 119:105

Your word is a lamp to my feet and a light to my path

Archbishop Nicholas Duncan-Williams

January-March 2016

DEVOTIONAL

THE
LAMP

Psalm 119:105
Your word is a lamp to my feet
And a light to my path

Archbishop Nicholas
DUNCAN-WILLIAMS

JANUARY - MARCH 2016

Devotional Guide by
Archbishop Nicholas Duncan-Williams.
ISSN: 2026 6952
Produced in Ghana by Rhema Publishers
Copyright © 2015 Rhema Publishers

Cover Design:
Create Bureau
Facebook: Create Bureau
Email: Createbureau@gamil.com
Tel: 0243937601

DOMINION TELEVISION
is now on air 24/7!

Catch us live on MultiTV channel 5
For more information on DTV
Call 0302.745.000 or visit
www.dominiontelevision.com
www.actionchapel.net

ACTION CHAPEL PRAYER CATHEDRAL

SERVICE TIMES

SPINTEX ROAD, ACCRA

SUNDAY MORNING SERVICES
7 am - 9:30 am
10 am - 12:30 pm

EVENING SERVICE
6 pm - 8:30 pm

WEDNESDAY (MIDWEEK) SERVICE:
6:30 pm - 8: 30 pm

DOMINION HOUR (Thursdays):
9 am - 12 noon.

MORNING GLORY (Saturdays):
7 am - 9:30 am.

FIRM FOUNDATION SUNDAY SERVICES:
7 am - 9:30 am
10 am - 12: 30 pm

RELEVANCE SUNDAY SERVICE:
3 pm – 4:30pm

For Action branches, fellowship,
and other church activities,
please call +233.302.745.000
or visit www.actionchapel.net

FOLLOW ME ON FACEBOOK!
https://www.facebook.com/archbishopduncanwilliams

Dear Friend,

Prophetic salutations in the name of Jesus Christ our soon coming King! On behalf of the Action Chapel International Family world-wide, I welcome you to a brand new year--Our Year of Restoration.

Reflecting over the past year, I realize that the year was a difficult one for most families. However, I am confident that you will not start the year slacking in faith because of the trying times you faced. In spite of the difficulties and challenges you went through, I want you to know that your comeback will be greater than your setback. Keep hope alive because I perceive that this is a year of unprecedented potentials and possibilities.

*What do you envision for yourself in the coming year? I see an endless stream of opportunities and open doors waiting for a man or woman of faith. The key here is holding on in faith and being sensitive to the promptings of the Holy Spirit. You have to believe that the God you serve is able to give you an upper hand in all situations and circumstances. All He needs from you is to agree with Him and have confidence in Him. The bible says in **Hebrews 10:35:***

Therefore do not cast away your confidence, which has great reward. For you have need of endurance, so that after you have done the will of God, you may receive the promise.

What is the will of God for your life this year? What are you dreaming about? Do not cast away your dreams.

Let the tenacity and persistence of the young man Joseph encourage you throughout the year. The bible says Joseph was a dreamer; he told his brothers about his big dreams but was persecuted by his brothers for his dreams. In spite of this persecution, his dreams were unstoppable. The bible recounts that he dreamed yet another dream. Refuse to let your dreams die because of setbacks. Restart that business, ministry/church or divine assignment. You cannot afford to lose hope because the best is yet to come! We know from Joseph's story that he suffered many setbacks from afflictions inflicted on him by those he loved. Despite the many years of affliction, he triumphed in honour and came to a season of rest. As you journey through the year, do not stop dreaming, keep hope alive because you are about to enter your season of rest in the name of Jesus.

I declare over your life that you will have the courage of a lion, the eye of an eagle, and the strength of a horse. You will have the upper hand, take dominion, run through troops and leap over walls. You will break iron bars and gates of bronze and regain lost territories. May your coast be enlarged and your land be blessed. I declare that you will re-possess your possessions in the name of Jesus!

May the Lord bless and establish you; may this New Year bring you honour, triumph and restoration in the name of Jesus.

Yours for new beginnings,
Archbishop Nicholas Duncan-Williams

THE LAMP

HOW TO APPROACH THE DEVOTION USING THIS NEW FORMAT

The new format of The Lamp is designed to make your quiet time even more fruitful. Before you start using the guide, take time to read and understand the rationale for the format and design. The critical elements of the new format are as follows:

1. **Creating Fellowship with God:** When you are always in the closet with God alone, you are not the author, the preacher, or the teacher of the word. It is an opportunity for you to experience real fellowship. Forget about worries, and be receptive to hearing from God. Fellowshipping with someone is a two-way activity which involves talking and listening. God will speak to you through the Scripture passages, memory verses and through the Holy Spirit. Your job is to listen. When it is your turn, you can pray, speak in tongues, or just meditate on His

word. God will listen. This is different from being in a church where you do all the listening and there is not much interaction with God. With continues practice, eventually you will develop the discipline of hearing from God.

2. **Knowledge of the Bible:** When you are ready for your devotion time, make sure you have your bible. This is not just a session of reading and praying. You may even have a small note book to record your experience with God or track your answers to prayers.

3. **Practical Application of the Word:** This section of the format ties the scripture passages with useful and practical application of the Word. You may or may not be able to relate to some of the situations presented, however, you will see helpful case scenarios which can serve as a guide in the present or the future.

4. **Take Time:** Do not rush to go through your devotion time. Each daily devotion is formatted to help you spend more time in the Word and prayer. You will not be blessed if you try to rush through it.

5. **Making it Personal:** This session of the devotional is very critical. If you skip it or hurry through it, you are not helping yourself. Please go through this session as prayerfully as you do the others.

6. **Prayer:** This section provides you space to write down your prayer request or to jot down any thoughts or notes you may have.

7. **Declarations:** No one can prepare declarations for you to repeat all the time. You have more insight into your personal situation and will also receive direction from the Holy Spirit on how you should pray. It is important for you to make your own declarations.

THE SPIRIT OF WORSHIP

Meditate on Psalm 96:1-9

> **Memorize Psalms 29:2**
>
> *"Ascribe to the LORD the glory due his name; worship the LORD in the splendor of holiness."*

Making it Real

Not too long ago, in typical Ghanaian families, the parental bedroom was considered a sacred place. Children were usually not allowed to enter under any circumstances. In addition, there were several household items which were specifically reserved for use by fathers alone. These were: cups, plates, even sometimes, a special chair. Even in the absence of fathers, these items were not touched in fear that you might get punished. This was because the father of the home was revered and honored. Likewise, in the Old Testament, God was honored, revered and was held in such high esteem that, they were not allowed to mention

God's name. They did not want to mention His name in vain.

In the New Testament dispensation however, we are free to mention the names of God. Unfortunately, as a result, people have become desensitized and the awe of God and His reverence has decreased over time. People have become very casual with the name of God and it has become the norm to take the Lord's name in vain.

Think about the first commandment and the prayer Jesus taught the disciples "Our Father". The first thing God asks of us is to give honor to and acknowledge His name. He does not want us to take His name in vain and we should not. Honoring God's name is an act of worship and obedience. Unless you have the Spirit of God within you, you cannot worship and honor God the way He deserves. This year, try to meditate on the goodness of God and all that He has done for you. I am sure that you have plenty of things that God has made provision for, plenty of things that God has delivered you from and most importantly--the gift of salvation. Enter the year 2016 with a spirit of worship, gratitude, and give honor to

whom honor is due—The Lord God in your
midst is mighty!

Making it Personal

What one specific truth is God teaching me today?

....

....

....

*One way to practically apply what God has taught
me today.*..

....

....

....

*What do I want to tell God today concerning what
He taught me?* [**My Prayer**] ....

....

....

....

My Personal Declaration for Today [*Write it **down
and speak it over and over***] ....

....

....

....

ENCOUNTERING GOD

Meditate on Jeremiah 9:23-24

> **Memorize** Psalm 71:8
>
> *"My mouth is filled with your praise, declaring your splendor all day long."*

Making it Real

Today, I want us to meditate on one of the strongest foundations of worship – experiencing the revelation of who God is. In Revelations, it states that angels sing, holy, holy, holy day and night. As they sing, the twenty-four elders also bow down and worship God. Once you are in the presence of God and sense God's awesomeness and glory you cannot help but to experience His splendor and worship our heavenly Father. Worship is an outward manifestation of your love, reverence, and submission to Him. Once you get to this revelation of who God is, you can never tire of giving Him worship. Many Christians today are not experiencing the privilege of a close unique relationship with God. If you have not experienced God on a personal level, then you cannot worship Him. The most you can do is to worship God with your lips. Our Heavenly Father wants us to know Him intimately and to worship Him with our hearts. Think about your daily activities and the other priorities of your life, how often do you carve out time in your day and go before God in worship?

Today, I want you to pause and take stock of what you experienced from God in 2015. Make a list of all of the things that God has done to demonstrate the manifestation of His presence in your life and give Him thanks and the worship that is due Him!

Making it Personal

What one specific truth is God teaching me today?

....

....

....

....

....

....

One way to practically apply what God has taught me today...

....

....

....

....

....

*What do I want to tell God today concerning what He taught me? [**My Prayer**]* ....

....

....

....

....

....

....

....

*My Personal Declaration for Today [**Write it down and speak it over and over**]* ....

....

....

....

....

....

....

COUNTING YOUR BLESSINGS

Take this opportunity to reflect over what you have learned in your interaction with God this week. It will be helpful if you write down your experiences

1. Of the lessons or truths God taught you this week, write down which one ministered to you above all the others? ....
   ....
   ....
   ....

2. Mention one experience you had this week that made that particular lesson or truth more real to you than before? ....
   ....
   ....
   ....

3. What was the verse that you were able to memorize out of the verses presented for the week? ....
   ....

....

....

4. Reflect over the lessons for the week.
**Pray and make the following Prophetic
Declarations** for the coming week

I give thanks unto the Lord for He is good
and His mercy endures forever.

I join the twenty four elders in worship,
crying holy, holy, holy Lord God Almighty,
who was, who is and who is to come. Worthy
art thou oh King of the universe.

I come into this New Year not in my name
but in the name of Jesus. Your word says
by strength shall no man prevail. I declare
therefore by divine authority, I prevail over
every contrary situation or circumstance
that will come against me this year in the
name of Jesus. I enter the year in power and
victory. I exercise dominion in the realms
of the Spirit and gain the upper hand in all
things throughout this year. This is my year
of elevation. This is my season. I rise up in
the power of the Holy Spirit and occupy my
set place in the year in the name of Jesus.

GOD'S WAY IS THE WAY

Meditate on Isaiah 55:6-9

> **Memorize** Psalm 14:12
>
> *"There is a way that appears to be right, but in the end it leads to death."*

Making it Real

Most people in the world have very strong opinions about who Jesus is. They have drawn their own conclusions about the significance of His presence on earth and unfortunately feel that they do not need a Savior. People come up with many excuses that attempt to explain why the Bible is outdated and no longer relevant. They claim that the bible is not in touch with the present issues of the day, they claim that the bible is discriminatory to women, or they even claim that the bible was written by men and therefore is discredited. Unfortunately, these people are relying on their own understanding, and intellectualism to justify their stance. Their pride will now allow them to submit

21

to and give honor to Christ. I am sure you have come across many people who have challenged your faith and tried to convince you that you are too religious, out-of-touch, or simply foolish for believing what the bible says. Or some people may try to convince you that you are in the wrong "religion". This simply illustrates that if we dwell on the opinions of men on an issue, we are likely to end up getting confused or discouraged. Acting as an ambassador for Christ in a "foreign" world (as this is not Jesus' Kingdom), can be pretty wearisome and a lonely experience. This is why it is so important to surround yourself with like-minded believers for encouragement and edification. In spite of all of the naysayers, and different arguments you hear against Christ, remember to always choose the narrow path. Jesus is the Way, the Truth, and the Life. Choose Jesus. Choose eternal life.

Making it Personal

What one specific truth is God teaching me today? ....
....
....

One way to practically apply what God has taught me today..

....

....

What do I want to tell God today concerning what He taught me? [**My Prayer**]..

....

....

My Personal Declaration for Today [**Write it down and speak it over and over**]..

....

....

SEEKING GOD'S DIRECTION

Meditate on Exodus 33:12-16

Memorize Psalms 25:4-5

Make me know Your ways, O LORD; Teach me Your paths. Lead me in Your truth and teach me, For You are the God of my salvation; For You I wait all the day.

Making it Real

Coming into the revelation of who God is—is not an automatic feat. God wants us to seek Him. His word encourages us that if we seek Him, we will find Him. Most of us lived very unhappy lives and were empty until we came into right relationship with Christ. We went on a journey of searching and searching until God revealed himself to us. Remember how the wise men from the east relentlessly travelled over forests and deserts until they found Baby Jesus. At that time, it was not possible for them to hear from Him. Now we are privileged because we live in the full dispensation of the Godhead – the Father, the Son and the Holy Spirit. As God's chosen ones, we are very privileged to have this awareness of who God is.

Not only does God want humanity to have a revelation of who He is, He also wants us to have a greater and deeper understanding of who He is, this is not possible if we remain complacent and stagnant in our walk with Jesus. We must continually seek God, study His word, and be on fire for Him. God does not want us to be lukewarm Christians.

Read through our passage for today and see what you can learn from Moses, the only man who is described as having spoken to God face to face. Where are you in your walk or search for God. Have you experienced a new and deeper, more intimate, relationship with Christ. Or are you still where you were several years ago? Have you sought direction from God? What is preventing you from having a face-to-face encounter with God?

Making it Personal

What one specific truth is God teaching me today? ....
....
....

One way to practically apply what God has taught me today..
....
....

*What do I want to tell God today concerning what He taught me? [**My Prayer**]* ....
....
....

*My Personal Declaration for Today [**Write it down and speak it over and over**]* ....
....
....

NO SHORT-SIGHTEDNESS

Meditate on 2 Peter 1:5-9

Memorize Revelation 3:17

"You say, 'I am rich; I have acquired wealth and do not need a thing.' But you do not realize that you are wretched, pitiful, poor, blind and naked."

Making it Real

Anyone who is familiar with elections and political campaigns in our country knows one sad occurrence that repeats itself over and over again. When elections draw near, politicians give money and other material things to a large portion of the electorate, specifically those who have not had access to a formal education. It has often been reported that some of them were given money usually about twenty Ghanaian cedis (about $6) which was enough to provide them incentive to vote for the politician.

Unfortunately, these individuals were only thinking about the present. They were seduced by the allurement of a three-square meal. They did not consider what would happen in the future when the corrupt politician they voted for would remain in office for several years. They did not consider that they would continue to live in a cycle of abject poverty which was not worth the 20 cedis they received for a meal that is long forgotten. God did not intend for man to live in such short-sightedness. God expects us to look far ahead. He does not want us to depend on ourselves, but at least He does not expect us to short-circuit the expectations for our lives. Does He not tell us that He even supplies more than we can think of or ask? When all our focus is on what we can have today, we become short-sighted and the Bible says we are blind.

Look beyond today because you do not know what God has placed out there for you. As a matter of fact, He has planted so many good things your way which takes long-term vision to see. If you focus on the present, you will lose sight of what God really wants to provide you in the future.

Making it Personal

What one specific truth is God teaching me today? ....
....
....

One way to practically apply what God has taught me today..
....
....

*What do I want to tell God today concerning what He taught me? [**My Prayer**]* ....
....
....

*My Personal Declaration for Today [**Write it down and speak it over and over**]* ....
....
....

ONE DAY AT A TIME

Meditate on Deuteronomy 7:20-24

Memorize Mathew 6:34

Therefore do not worry about tomorrow, for tomorrow will worry about itself. Each day has enough trouble of its own.

Making it Real

Today's passage is so significant in that it sets the tone for us to understand how God works with us. According to Genesis, God created the world in six days. Although He could have instantly created the world He chose to do it one day at a time. You have to understand the God we are dealing with. He does things systematically. He is not in a hurry; He is not in competition with anyone. He takes His time to build--brick by brick and layer upon layer until His work is perfectly done. Once it is completed, everyone will marvel at the completed project. It should not surprise anyone that the same principle applies to His children. Today, most people do not want to wait on God. Everyone is in a hurry. You should know by now that you cannot manipulate God or try to hurry God to give you what you want when you want it. From generation to generation, God perfectly orchestrated everything in His own perfect timing. See how long it took for Jesus Christ to manifest in the flesh? In between the promise in Genesis 3:15 to its fulfillment in the gospels, so many things happened during the existence of humanity. It was all a part of His plan. Today it is easier for us to believe in Jesus because of the long history of His proclamation and the shadows of His existence since the beginning of time.

Think about any goals you may have or the secret desires of your heart that you have been praying about; have you considered that perhaps God has already heard that prayer and perfecting the answer?

Making it Personal

What one specific truth is God teaching me today? ....
....

....
....
....
....

One way to practically apply what God has taught me today..
....
....
....

*What do I want to tell God today concerning what He taught me? [**My Prayer**]* ....
....
....
....

*My Personal Declaration for Today [**Write it down and speak it over and over**]* ....
....
....
....

LIGHT ON OUR PATH

Meditate on Psalm 119:105-112

> **Memorize** John 8:12
>
> *"When Jesus spoke again to the people, he said, "I am the light of the world. Whoever follows me will never walk in darkness, but will have the light of life."*

Making it Real

Driving on a highway (motorway) can be real fun with the presence of streetlights. Street lights that enable you to see at least 100 meters ahead do a lot to enhance driving in the night. Can you imagine driving on a highway where you only rely on the highlights from your vehicle? You are forced to drive with extra, extra care. The situation is critical in our part of the world where you cannot guarantee the state of the highway you are driving on; where you may unexpectedly meet potholes and speed ramps.

Your experience on the highway is easier in comparison to the journey of life. In life, you cannot guarantee what lies ahead. No matter how much planning you might do, you never know when an unexpected hurdle might appear. During those times, you will need much more than "physical light" to guide your path. You will need general guidelines and specific information concerning the paths you should take. This is when the presence of the Holy Spirit is necessary. He takes the word of God and enables you to see ahead. The Holy Spirit makes God's word the light onto your path and the lamp unto your feet.

How would you categorize a Christian who has no daily interaction with the Holy Spirit? He definitely would be walking in darkness. Every Christian must understand that without the light of God shining your path, you would be heading towards a headlong collision with the forces of darkness and you would not be able to see the wiles of the enemy. Why walk in darkness when you are the light of the world?

Making it Personal

What one specific truth is God teaching me today? ....

....

....

....

One way to practically apply what God has taught me today...

....

....

....

*What do I want to tell God today concerning what He taught me? [**My Prayer**]* ....

....

....

....

*My Personal Declaration for Today [**Write it down and speak it over and over**]* ....

....

....

....

SOW IN GOOD TIMING

Meditate on Ecclesiastes 3:1-8

> **Memorize** Genesis 8:22
>
> *"While the earth remains, seedtime and harvest, cold and heat, summer and winter, day and night, shall not cease."*

Making it Real

Our country is often described as an agricultural country. The truth is that if we strategically harnessed our natural resources for crop production, we would be in a position to feed ourselves, our neighbors and still have plenty for export. Our farmers in rural settings need recognition for the good work they have done over the years, especially knowing that many of them do not have access to technology in farming. They usually watch the weather. They know when to plant and when to wait. Sometimes when there is a false start of the planting season, experienced farmers know they should not sow their seeds. There is one big lesson the believer can learn from the local, peasant farmers waiting for the proper time. How can we take advantage of the wisdom of the farmer?

Whatever burning desire you have in your heart must be birthed at the right time. The right timing will ensure the full development of your vision. This does not happen by chance. When you present your vision and the desires of your heart before our Heavenly Father, He will know how to order your steps and create the most favorable circumstances for your vision to come into fruition. He will prepare the heart of the people who should invest in your business; He will bring the skilled labor you will need to help the business operate. He knows when the economy is doing well; and He also provides the good soil for you to plant for effective productivity.

There is a proper time and a proper place to do everything. All you have to do is trust God and wait for His perfect timing. He wants to see you succeed. Are you willing to allow God to take the lead?

Making it Personal

What one specific truth is God teaching me today? ....
....
....
....

One way to practically apply what God has taught me today ....
....
....
....

*What do I want to tell God today concerning what He taught me? [**My Prayer**]* ....
....
....
....

*My Personal Declaration for Today [**Write it down and speak it over and over**]* ....
....
....
....

COUNTING YOUR BLESSINGS

Take this opportunity to reflect over what you have learned in your interaction with God this week. It will be helpful if you write down your experiences

1. Of the lessons or truths God taught you this week, write down which one ministered to you above all the others?

   ....
   ....
   ....
   ....

2. Mention one experience you had this week that made that particular lesson or truth more real to you than before?

   ....
   ....
   ....
   ....

3. What was the verse that you were able to memorize out of the verses presented for the week? ....

....

....

....

4. Reflect over the lessons for the week. Pray and make the following Prophetic Declarations for the coming week

Holy Spirit, I thank you for guiding me into all truth. I refuse to lean on my own understanding. I trust in the wisdom and divine counsel of God.

I look beyond the challenges I face today and I lean on your everlasting arms in the name of Jesus.

Daily, the Lord will guide and protect my household and I from all forms all evil.

I will wait upon the Lord who is worthy to be praised. He will sustain my heart.

When my enemies and my foes rise up to eat my flesh they will stumble and fall.

Turn my captivity oh Lord like streams in the Negev. I declare that because I sow in tears I will reap in joy in the name of Jesus.

DISCOVER YOUR PURPOSE

Meditate on Genesis 12:1-4

> **Memorize** Jeremiah 1:4-5
>
> *"Then the word of the Lord came unto me, saying, Before I formed thee in the belly I knew thee; and before thou camest forth out of the womb I sanctified thee, and I ordained thee a prophet unto the nations."*

Making it Real

Many people have their own ways of defining and measuring success. However, I would like you to think of success from a different perspective. Success is often thought of as achieving your personal goals, whether financial, business, academic, etc. This definition is accurate, however, success is not just determined by your concrete personal goals. You might take a step back and think that you have successfully accomplished all that you set out to do, however, if God were to take inventory of your life would He be pleased?

There is a huge difference between God's call on your life versus your own personal goals. As a child of God, you have been created for His purpose. You will have to give an account of your life and the choices you made. Your life has to be lived out purposefully with divine appointments, divine relationships, and seasons. You cannot blindly move forward without praying and seeking God's face regarding the various choices in life you have to make whether it's where you will live, the spouse you will choose, the profession you will pursue etc. The Word of God clearly states that your steps have been ordered. Your success is really defined by fulfilling God's vision and purpose for your life.

Meditate again on God's declaration to Abraham in our passage for today. It was about God's purpose for Abraham.

If all you did was to acquire great wealth and property, do you think that this alone would please God? Take some time to examine the motives behind your goals. Would God approve? Are you on the right path?

Making it Personal

What one specific truth is God teaching me today? ....
....
....
....

One way to practically apply what God has taught me today...
....
....
....

What do I want to tell God today concerning what He taught me? [***My Prayer***] ....
....
....
....

My Personal Declaration for Today [***Write it down and speak it over and over***] ....
....
....
....

EQUIPPED TO SUCCEED

Meditate on Exodus 31:1-10

Memorize 1 Corinthians 7:7

"Yet I wish that all men were even as I myself am However, each man has his own gift from God, one in this manner, and another in that."

Making it Real

Today's passage is about the design of Aaron's robe for ministry. The passage clearly states that God appointed specific individuals to assist Moses and filled them with the necessary wisdom, understanding, knowledge and all kinds of skills to do what Moses commanded. It was not Moses who designed the robe. God gave clear instructions to Moses that Aholiab should do the designing. Moses did exactly what God had required of Him and delegated special tasks to those whom God had specifically chosen.

Experts in communication will tell you that when information passes from one person to the other, deterioration of its content begins immediately. This means that it is even possible that the first person who heard the first instruction may have already missed portions of it. How then was it that Aholiab was able to design the robe according to the exact specifications required by God? It is simple – He was an expert. The word "expert" today is what God would rightfully call the spirit of wisdom and understanding. When God asked Moses to ask Aholiab to design the robe, God had already equipped him with wisdom and understanding in that specific area. God does not assign people tasks unless He equips them for it!

When you discover your purpose, know that God has already equipped you with what you will need for success. You must discover these gifts and talents that He has given you and develop them so that you can fulfill your purpose.

Making it Personal

What one specific truth is God teaching me today? ....
....
....
....

One way to practically apply what God has taught me today ....
....
....
....

*What do I want to tell God today concerning what He taught me? [**My Prayer**]* ....
....
....
....

*My Personal Declaration for Today [**Write it down and speak it over and over**]* ....
....
....
....

HAVING A JOURNEYING MENTALITY

Meditate on Exodus 3:10-17

> **Memorize** Matthew 24:12-13
>
> *"And because iniquity shall abound, the love of many shall wax cold. But he that shall endure unto the end, the same shall be saved."*

Making it Real

By now I am sure we understand the difference between achievement and success. Achievement is a one-time event. Success spans over a period time and is closely-linked with your purpose for life. Every journey has a beginning, and follows a path until it gets to the end. During the journey, there may be obstacles, hindrances, and distractions which often threaten the completion of the journey and may tempt the traveler to think of quitting or returning to where he started.

Today's passage informs us that when God called Moses, He told him He was calling him to embark on a journey ending in the Promised Land. This is why God raised Joshua after Moses' death because the journey was not yet completed.

Discovering your purpose in life is just the beginning of one long journey that ends only when your time on earth is done. Many people had dreams in life and somehow have given up on the way. To complete your purpose in life, you need a journey mentality, not an achievement mentality. If you do not have a journey mentality, it is difficult to cope with the challenges of this life. This is when the tendency to quit becomes tempting. Sometimes even pastors who believed they were called to engage in spiritual ministry cut short their journey. What is your mindset towards fulfilling God's purpose for your life? Are you in for the long haul?

Making it Personal

What one specific truth is God teaching me today? ....
....

....
....

One way to practically apply what God has taught me today..
....
....
....

What do I want to tell God today concerning what He taught me? [***My Prayer***]..
....
....
....

My Personal Declaration for Today [***Write it down and speak it over and over***]......................................
....
....
....

KNOW YOURSELF

Meditate on Romans 12:3-8

Memorize Ephesians 4:7

"But unto every one of us is given grace according to the measure of the gift of Christ."

Making it Real

Most 100 meter runners also run in the 200 meter race, like Usain Bolt has done in the past. In the International Association of Athletics Federations (IAAF) championship in Beijing in 2015, Shelly Ann Fraser Pryce realized that if she trained for both 200 meter and 100 meter races, it would affect her performance in the 100 meter dash which she was determined to win; so she declined participating in the 200 meters race. Just as she anticipated, she won the women's 100 meters race. Frazer-Pryce demonstrated one fundamental truth that is critical in attaining success – knowing yourself.

When you know yourself well, you know both your strengths and weaknesses. That reality does not change the truth that we can do all things through Christ who strengthens us. You know that if you have not learnt to fly an aircraft, you cannot say you can do all things through Christ who strengthens you and get the world's top evangelist or faith preacher let you fly a plane he or she is traveling on. It will not happen.

Although by virtue of the indwelling Holy Spirit you can potentially do anything, in His sovereign will God decided that no man should be able to do everything and do all very well. That is why He multiplied Himself severally in us as per our passage for today.

The wise Christian is the one who knows himself and knows at any point in time what he can handle and what he cannot. The grace of God works best with the gift that God has equipped you with, and not the gift you do not have. This explains why God spoke to Moses to allow another man to design Aaron's robe. Dear Christian, know yourself so you do not make a mess and make a shipwreck of your faith.

Making it Personal

What one specific truth is God teaching me today? ....
....
....
....

One way to practically apply what God has taught me today ....
....
....
....

*What do I want to tell God today concerning what He taught me? [**My Prayer**]* ....
....
....
....

*My Personal Declaration for Today [**Write it down and speak it over and over**]* ....
....
....
....

WALK IN YOUR PATH

Meditate on 2 Timothy 2:1-7

Memorize 1 Corinthians 7:17

Nevertheless, each person should live as a believer in whatever situation the Lord has assigned to them, just as God has called them. This is the rule I lay down in all the churches.

Making it Real

In every competition there are rules and regulations which should be followed. If you adhere to the rules and eventually win, you are honored. In the past and presently, there have been several instances of athletes being disqualified because they were found guilty of using strength-enhancing drugs. As a result, some were stripped of their medals after investigations proved they cheated   One immediate disqualifier in competitions is cheating. Your position in the game will be forfeited without any questions. Some of these same rules apply in life as well. You cannot cheat and cut corners to get ahead. You cannot undermine another person's position, gifts, or talents to push your own agenda.

There are many individuals who will try at all costs to become something that they are not. Or perhaps they are trying to fulfill someone else's agenda to please them; perhaps they have lied and cheated to move ahead. This simply means they are not fulfilling God's true purpose for their lives. Do not get caught up in status and image and do not covet another person's position or gifts. Your purpose is to ensure that you are fulfilling God's destiny for your life. If you think you are on the wrong track, it is never too late. Let the Holy Spirit lead you in the right direction.

Making it Personal

What one specific truth is God teaching me today? ....
....
....
....

One way to practically apply what God has taught me today..

....

....

....

What do I want to tell God today concerning what He taught me? [**My Prayer**] ....

....

....

....

My Personal Declaration for Today [**Write it down and speak it over and over**] ....

....

....

....

BE A PROBLEM SOLVER

Meditate on 1 Samuel 17:31-37

Memorize Daniel 11:32

"And such as do wickedly against the covenant shall he corrupt by flatteries: but the people that do know their God shall be strong, and do exploits."

Making it Real

What happens when a country is confronted by a problem and no one seems to have a solution? This was the case when Israel was being confronted and bullied by a giant and it appeared that no one had a solution. The Israelites were paralyzed with fear. Suddenly, David appeared on the scene and asked what would be done for the man who provided the solution. Initially, because of his youth and stature no one took him seriously but with persistence he finally got a chance to prove himself.

If you follow the story, you realize that everyone expected David to apply methods that were familiar; methods that have been proven over the years – military might. Anyone who knows the end of the story knows that David used a means that was not the norm. He used a method that no one in Israel had thought about – pray and invite God into the situation.

Year after year our country is faced with so many issues needing extraordinary interventions. We need more leaders like David on the scene. Not just to solve security or military problems, but to provide solutions for our governance, economy, education, trade and commerce etc. Now that corruption has invaded all various sectors of national life; the need for problem solvers has become more critical.

Perhaps there is a giant in your marriage, in your family, in your city, or your nation, has it occurred to you that if you availed yourself God can use you as well?

Making it Personal

What one specific truth is God teaching me today? ....
....
....
....

One way to practically apply what God has taught me today..
....
....
....

*What do I want to tell God today concerning what He taught me? [**My Prayer**]* ....
....
....
....

*My Personal Declaration for Today [**Write it down and speak it over and over**]*..
....
....
....

COUNTING YOUR BLESSINGS

> *Take this opportunity to reflect over what you have learned in your interaction with God this week. It will be helpful if you write down your experiences*

1. Of the lessons or truths God taught you this week, write down which one ministered to you above all the others?

   ....
   ....
   ....
   ....

2. Mention one experience you had this week that made that particular lesson or truth more real to you than before?

   ....
   ....
   ....
   ....

3. What was the verse that you were able to memorize out of the verses presented for

the week? ....
....
....
....

4. Reflect over the lessons for the week. Pray and make the following Prophetic Declarations for the coming week

Oh Lord, open my eyes to see the purpose for which you created me; a purpose that will bring you honor and glory in the name of Jesus.

I declare that because you called me you have divinely equipped me with every spiritual blessings in heavenly places in Christ Jesus.

As I travel on this journey of life, I use all the gifts and talents you have given me to bring you glory.

I declare that any personality that will attempt to subvert my course is arrested, bound and cast out in the name of Jesus.

I will accomplish my God given assignment by divine authority in the name of Jesus.

DO NOT FORGET GOD

Meditate on Deuteronomy 8:10-18

> **Memorize** Hebrews 11:6
>
> *"But without faith it is impossible to please Him: for he that cometh to God must believe that He is, and that he is a Rewarder of them that diligently seek Him."*

Making it Real

It is not uncommon for people to become complacent with their relationship with God and eventually regulate Him to the background. Some people stop coming to church or stop praying as soon as God blesses them with an answer to their prayers. Satan is very strategic because this occurrence does not happen overnight. It may begin with missing a church service or two, getting caught up with your career or a relationship with another man or woman or perhaps the cares of the world until eventually, God has been omitted out of your life.

We cannot seek God only when we need Him or want something. God desires to have a long-lasting intimate relationship with us. Do you think that you can deceive God when you pursue Him for your own selfish purposes as opposed to earnestly pursuing His presence in your life?

The Bible admonishes us to give honor where honor is due; but it appears we run with the little that He gives us and in the process forget Him. Think about your relationship with God, where have you fallen short, been too busy, or simply have not acknowledged His grace and goodness in your life? People who forget God allow themselves to be open to temptations and forsake the blessings that God desires to shower upon them. Do not be foolish and remember to diligently seek your Father in Heaven.

Making it Personal

What one specific truth is God teaching me today? ....

....

....

....

One way to practically apply what God has taught me today...
....
....
....

*What do I want to tell God today concerning what He taught me? [**My Prayer**]*...
....
....
....

*My Personal Declaration for Today [**Write it down and speak it over and over**]*......................................
....
....
....

WATCH AND PRAY

Meditate on Genesis 4:6-7

Memorize 1 Corinthians 10:12-13

"So, if you think you are standing firm, be careful that you don't fall! No temptation has overtaken you except what is common to mankind. And God is faithful; he will not let you be tempted beyond what you can bear. But when you are tempted, he will also provide a way out so that you can endure it."

Making it Real

Watch and pray is a common phrase in the Christian faith. In fact, it is often more applicable in spiritual warfare than in other aspects of the Christian life. Praying involves having a conversation with our heavenly Father concerning our daily lives and ensuring the fulfillment of His kingdom here on earth. To watch means to observe, to pay attention to, and to be alert.

Jesus admonished us to watch and to pray--meaning that we cannot be ignorant of the devices of the enemy when he is always looking for an opportunity to devour us. The complacent Christian is an easy victim of temptations, traps, snares, and unexpected trials and mishaps. Refer to today's passage, why do you think God was warning Cain? How does this compare to Paul's exhortation in 1 Corinthians 10:12-13?

Thank God that even in the midst of temptation, He provides a way of escape. If we remain watchful, we will be delivered from many instances of temptations and snares.

Making it Personal

What one specific truth is God teaching me today? ....

....

....

....

One way to practically apply what God has taught me today ....

....

....
....

What do I want to tell God today concerning what He taught me? [**My Prayer**] ....
....
....
....

My Personal Declaration for Today [**Write it down and speak it over and over**] ....
....
....
....

STAND YOUR GROUND
Meditate on Acts 4:13-22

Memorize 1 Peter 3:15-16

"But in your hearts revere Christ as Lord. Always be prepared to give an answer to everyone who asks you to give the reason for the hope that you have. But do this with gentleness and respect, keeping a clear conscience, so that those who speak maliciously against your good behavior in Christ may be ashamed of their slander."

Making it Real

"In Kentucky, the Rowan County clerk sits in jail for refusing to obey the Constitution while claiming she answers to "a higher power" of fundamentalist Christian religion. Is she a threat to America? Damn right she is, along with the Bible-spouting fanatics who claim Armageddon is coming in a fiery Judgment Day where God almighty will strike down the sinners who follow the law of the land. They promote purported claims of advocating

religion over all else. Hard line fundamentalists claim gay marriage, legal abortion and everything from premarital sex to a threat of immigration will bring an angry God coming to earth to lay waste on those who don't heed the call".

This is an excerpt from an article that came on the internet on September 8, 2015 by one Doug Thompson, entitled, "The terrorism of 'God's law"

County Clerk Davis was sent to jail for a few days because she decided that she would listen to God and not man. This is one of many such incidences that we are about to witness in the world in these last days. This is similar to what is in our passage for today. Under such circumstances the believer has one option – to stand his ground. Standing your ground is not just about making declarations to the devil in prayer. A greater component of standing our ground in these last days has to do with giving a reason for what we believe and doing what the three Hebrew boys did. Having done all... stand!

Making it Personal

What one specific truth is God teaching me today? ....
....
....
....

One way to practically apply what God has taught me today ....
....
....
....

*What do I want to tell God today concerning what He taught me? [**My Prayer**]* ....
....
....
....

*My Personal Declaration for Today [**Write it down and speak it over and over**]* ....
....
....
....

MAKING FASTING MEANINGFUL

Meditate on James 4:4-10

Memorize Matthew 6:16-18

"When you fast, do not look somber as the hypocrites do, for they disfigure their faces to show others they are fasting. Truly I tell you, they have received their reward in full. But when you fast, put oil on your head and wash your face, so that it will not be obvious to others that you are fasting, but only to your Father, who is unseen; and your Father, who sees what is done in secret, will reward you."

Making it Real

It is very clear that fasting has always been associated with prayer. They go hand in hand. Although prayer can stand alone, fasting needs to be supplemented with the power of prayer otherwise there will be no spiritual results.

There are many ways a fast can be done. Some people may fast from sweets, and abstain from certain types of food or activities. The length of the fast can vary as well. Some people may be led by the Holy Spirit to fast for a half a day, a few days, or even a few weeks.

Most importantly, fasting is really about denying the flesh for a season and drawing closer to God. It should not be reduced to a routine or a ritual. When you begin a fast, you have to understand why you are doing it so that it can be an effective spiritual exercise. Jesus began our Scripture for today with "When you fast" not "If you fast". From the Scripture we can infer that it is a given that Christians should be fasting. There are certain obstacles, strongholds, etc. that will not break unless you fast and pray. Do not miss out on the benefits of this spiritual exercise.

If you have never fasted before, this is your opportunity to build yourself up spiritually. Do not miss out on the opportunity to see how God can manifest Himself in your life and in your personal situation. What is Jesus trying to teach about fasting in today's memory verse?

Making it Personal

What one specific truth is God teaching me today? ....
....
....
....

One way to practically apply what God has taught me today ....
....
....
....

*What do I want to tell God today concerning what He taught me? [**My Prayer**]* ....
....
....
....

*My Personal Declaration for Today [**Write it down and speak it over and over**]* ....
....
....
....

MORE THAN A CONQUEROR

Meditate on Hebrews 2:5-9

Memorize Romans 8:36-37

"As it is written, for your sake we face death all day long; we are considered as sheep to be slaughtered." No, in all these things we are more than conquerors through him who loved us."

Making it Real

What does it mean when the Bible describes us as more than conquerors? The strong suggestion is that there is a conqueror, and then there is one who is then described as being more than the conqueror. The common explanation to this is that the conqueror goes to battle, fights hard, and bravely goes through the unfavorable circumstances of war until it's over. When his work is done and the victory is won, a second person is invited and given the full rights of benefit of the spoils of the war.

The person invited to enjoy the full benefits of the war did not lift a finger when the war was going on. As a matter of fact he may not even be around when the battles were being fought. He wakes up one day and is handed a legal document of inheritance, spelling his rights and privileges of spoils of a war he did not fight.

From heaven when the war broke out, Jesus was there to cast Lucifer out. From Genesis to the time Jesus came, evil continued to wage war against the good that God did for us. Today's passage summarizes Jesus' eternal victory for us. Read through that again.

The victory for the battle of life has already been won for us by Jesus. The bullets of the enemy that hit us can best be likened to rubber bullets that have no piercing power. The truth is we are fighting from victory unto victory. We are already winners in Christ. Reflect your attitudes over the past week and evaluate in which situations you refused to think like "more than a conqueror" pray that you never do that to yourself again. Determine to be who God says you are.

Making it Personal

What one specific truth is God teaching me today? ....

....

....

....

One way to practically apply what God has taught me today...

....

....

....

*What do I want to tell God today concerning what He taught me? [**My Prayer**]* ....

....

....

....

*My Personal Declaration for Today [**Write it down and speak it over and over**]* ....

....

....

....

NO TURNING BACK
Meditate on Luke 9:57-62

Memorize Hebrews 10:38-39

"But my righteous one will live by faith. And I take no pleasure in the one who shrinks back. But we do not belong to those who shrink back and are destroyed, but to those who have faith and are saved."

Making it Real

When long distance athletes run in a competition they run until they have crossed the finished line. Their intention is to continue going without stopping. They cannot turn back once the race begins. Those who run in the steeple chase have to jump over obstacles intentionally placed in their path. Even with the obstacles they continue to run. This is similar to the Christian life.

During your walk as a Christian, you will run into snares, traps, obstacles, and distractions.

You may get discouraged and decide you no longer want to continue the path. You may lose things along the way, family, friends, and valuable possessions. You may end up coming to a crossroads where you have to decide if you will continue along the same path or trust God for the new one. All of these aforementioned hurdles or challenges are meant to strengthen you, and or test you!

At some point, you will ask yourself is this really worth the struggle? You may question why all of these things are happening to you. When the Israelites were fleeing Egypt and God was preparing a new life for them, they began to murmur and complain about their situation and actually wished that they were back in Egypt. They wanted to go back to what they knew and were familiar with. It may be tempting for you to go back to your old way of life, however, God wants you to forget about the past and focus on the new thing He is doing in your life. When you find yourself getting discouraged do not look at your situation, your obstacles, and the distractions, focus on God and do not turn back!

Making it Personal

What one specific truth is God teaching me today? ....
....
....
....

One way to practically apply what God has taught me today..
....
....
....

*What do I want to tell God today concerning what He taught me? [**My Prayer**]* ....
....
....
....

*My Personal Declaration for Today [**Write it down and speak it over and over**]*..
....
....
....

COUNTING YOUR BLESSINGS

Take this opportunity to reflect over what you have learned in your interaction with God this week. It will be helpful if you write down your experiences

1. Of the lessons or truths God taught you this week, write down which one ministered to you above all the others?

   ....
   ....
   ....
   ....

2. Mention one experience you had this week that made that particular lesson or truth more real to you than before?

   ....
   ....
   ....
   ....

3. What was the verse that you were able to memorize out of the verses presented for the week? ....
....
....
....

4. Reflect over the lessons for the week. **Pray and make the following Prophetic Declarations** for the coming week

I declare that by the grace of God; I will not forget God. As I manifest His grace and favor over my life I will remember that it is not by my strength.

I overcome through the blood of Jesus all obstacles on the way to my desired place.

I activate the power of God over my life through fasting and prayer and declare that I am more than a conqueror through Him who loved me.

As I watch and pray, I break through all barriers and declare, I take my position and stand till I receive my breakthrough in the name of Jesus.

UNDERSTANDING GRACE

Meditate on 2 Corinthians 12:1-10

Memorize Hebrews 4:16

"Let us then with confidence draw near to the throne of grace, that we may receive mercy and find grace in the time of need."

Making it Real

Unfortunately, for many Christians the phrase "by God's grace" has become a cliché. People usually use this phrase to acknowledge whatever blessing they have experienced as a result of God's Divine intervention. This is one example of grace. Grace is also experiencing mercy, compassion, and receiving God's provision just because He loves us.

Other times you may have gone through hardships, trials, and temptations. During this time, you may have learned many things such as longsuffering, patience, faith and the like. The only way you managed to endure them was to experience God's supernatural grace.

This is exactly what the Apostle Paul is trying to draw our attention to in the memory verse above. Grace enables you to develop Christian character; grace gives you the power to overcome temptation; Grace gives you power to hold on in difficult times; Grace enables you to do what everyone thinks cannot be done; and finally grace makes you bold in the face of challenging circumstances of life.

Do you now understand how Christians are able to conquer and overcome the challenges of life? The average individual without God's intervention would probably succumb to the temptations and have a constant negative outlook. Think about your trials, tribulations, and times when things seemed impossible to overcome. How much of God's grace was evident during those times?

Making it Personal

What one specific truth is God teaching me today?

....

....

....

....

One way to practically apply what God has taught me today...

....

....

....

What do I want to tell God today concerning what He taught me? [**My Prayer**]................................

....

....

....

My Personal Declaration for Today [**Write it down and speak it over and over**] ....

....

....

....

GOD IS FAITHFUL
Meditate on 2 Timothy 1:6-12

> **Memorize** Deuteronomy 7:9
>
> *"Know therefore that the LORD your God is God, the faithful God who keeps covenant and steadfast love with those who love him and keep his commandments, to a thousand generations."*

Making it Real

How many times have you trusted someone to provide, follow through, or be there for you during difficult times? How many broken promises have you given or experienced? You may have had high hopes and expectations of people who were extremely close to you—only to have been let you down when you needed them the most. This, unfortunately, is the reality of life. Most of us have not figured out yet that it is only in the Lord Jesus Christ that our hope will never be cut off. There are several examples of God's promises to us in His word that are unconditional.

In spite of the fact the men and women are fallible they still continually struggle to take God at His word. They would rather place confidence in parents, scholars, philosophers, or prophets. We have to realize that our hope is not found in men who are imperfect and who do not have all the answers. We need to learn how to place all of our hopes, fears, desires, and trust into a God who is infallible and always available. Think about some areas in your life that you may be struggling with. How has God demonstrated His faithfulness to you in those areas?

Making it Personal

What one specific truth is God teaching me today?

....

....

....

....

One way to practically apply what God has taught me today...

....

....
....

*What do I want to tell God today concerning what He taught me? [**My Prayer**]* ....
....
....
....
....

*My Personal Declaration for Today [**Write it down and speak it over and over**]* ....
....
....
....
....

GOD HAS FINAL AUTHORITY

Meditate on Matthew 16:13-20

> **Memorize** Isaiah 55:11
>
> *"So is my word that goes out from my mouth: It will not return to me empty, but will accomplish what I desire and achieve the purpose for which I sent it"*

Making it Real

It is not unusual for people to take a look at your circumstances, your status, your skill set and to make a final judgment based upon their personal opinion. Unfortunately, many individuals take the opinions of others and agree with them. Instead of taking a stand and hoping for the best, they accept "reality" and prepare for the worst. I once read a book in which a pastor described the difference between the facts versus the truth. This was such an eye-opener for me. He stated that although the facts may point in one direction that appears to be final, you cannot focus on the facts. You have to focus on the truth regarding your situation. That truth is the Word of God—what does the truth say about your situation? Jesus Christ is the Author and the Finisher of our faith and His Word always has the final say in our lives—not man, not your enemy. So even when your situation looks bleak, hopeless, dead, and unchangeable, the truth and the real fact of the matter is that with God there is nothing impossible!

God can turn any situation around. Sometimes you may have people in your life who are "realists" and may tell you to consider the facts in your situation—perhaps your spouse has left and stated that he/she is not coming back, perhaps your doctor has told you that there is no cure for your illness, perhaps it appears that your son or daughter may never come to Christ. The truth of the matter is that when you apply God's Word to your situation, He has the final say—not the facts and not man! So be encouraged and place your trust in His Word—not the opinions of man.

Making it Personal

What one specific truth is God teaching me today?

....

....

....

....

....

One way to practically apply what God has taught me today..

....

....

....

*What do I want to tell God today concerning what He taught me? [**My Prayer**]* ....

....

....

....

*My Personal Declaration for Today [**Write it down and speak it over and over**]* ....

....

....

....

....

THE EARTH IS GOD'S FOOTSTOOL

Meditate on Isaiah 45:18-19

Memorize Isaiah 66:1-2

"This is what the Lord says: "Heaven is my throne, and the earth is my footstool. Where is the house you will build for me? Where will my resting place be? Has not my hand made all these things, and so they came into being?" declares the Lord."

Making it Real

In the publication, We Are Not Alone In Universe, NASA Scientists reported the possibility of other earth-like planets in our universe. "It's highly improbable in the limitless vastness of the universe that we humans stand alone," the report said. NASA experts are saying, and we may be close to finding alien life. In fact, they think it may happen in the next two decades.

Space experts are talking about the search for earth-like planets that host life.

What have they been thinking all these years? Who said the earth is the only planet referred to in the Genesis story? God's creation is yet to be fully discovered. If all these were a result of the big bang, then it really must be big, from nowhere, no origin, no cause, no one behind it – how miserable humanity must be in thinking we know it all.

The earth is described as God's footstool; so the question is where does He sit to rest His foot on the earth? We can go on and on and raise those questions, all of which point to the fact that God is unsearchable. We will not be able to fully grasp His greatness. The symbols used in the Bible themselves are not adequate to describe God; and that has been the struggle of the world's philosophers and scientists. God cannot occupy any human mind. He is too big for that!

Making it Personal

What one specific truth is God teaching me today?

....

....

....
....

One way to practically apply what God has taught me today...
....
....
....
....

*What do I want to tell God today concerning what He taught me? [**My Prayer**]* ....
....
....
....
....

*My Personal Declaration for Today [**Write it down and speak it over and over**]*...............................
....
....
....
....

GOD RULES ON EARTH

Meditate on Daniel 4:19-27

Memorize Psalm 47:7-9

"For God is the King of all the earth; sing to him a psalm of praise. God reigns over the nations; God is seated on his holy throne. The nobles of the nations assemble as the people of the God of Abraham, for the kings of the earth belong to God; He is greatly exalted."

Making it Real

As we experience and witness the violence occurring in America, the airstrikes in Libya, the natural disasters which claim thousands of lives, and the political unrest in many countries around the world, one might wonder where God is in all of this.

Does God really exist and if He does—why is not He doing something? Others might think that God does not care and that He is not in control. However, this is far from the truth. God is very much aware about what is happening in our lives and does want to get involved. He is waiting for us!

Before the fall, man had total and complete dominion over the earth. As a result of sin, man's fellowship with God was broken and the earth became cursed. In order for us to be reconciled to God and our dominion over the earth restored, we had to rely on Jesus' atonement for the sins of the world through the Cross. The Blood of Jesus' Christ justified us and as a result we are able re-enforce our dominion over the earth which was God's original intention. So our responsibility is to cry out and pray and to ask God to enforce His will upon the earth. God will not interfere unless we ask Him to!

No matter how bleak things may seem, even when things appear as if our enemies are victorious, God is always in control and always has the final Word. He knows the beginning and the end; He is the Author and the Finisher and the God of the Universe. So even in the midst of confusion and the supposed "chaos" Jesus promised us peace. Not as the world gives, but His peace the peace that surpasses all understanding. Read our passage for today and be reassured that God reigns over all!

Making it Personal

What one specific truth is God teaching me today?

....

....

....

One way to practically apply what God has taught me today...

....

....

....

What do I want to tell God today concerning what He taught me? [***My Prayer***] ....

....

....

....

My Personal Declaration for Today [***Write it down and speak it over and over***] ....

....

....

GOD FIGHTS FOR YOU

Meditate on Exodus 14:10-14

Memorize Isaiah 59:19

"So shall they fear the name of the LORD from the west, and his glory from the rising of the sun. When the enemy shall come in like a flood, the Spirit of the LORD shall lift up a standard against him."

Making it Real

We are living in days which are not going to be easy for the believer to live as a Christian. From internal conflicts with character development to external challenges, the reality of being confronted with spiritual battles is becoming more evident. The chaos in the world also adds its own pressure. We cannot ignore and say that we are immune to the killings in Syria, Iraq, Afghanistan, or to natural disasters and earthquakes in several parts of the world, or to the decline of faith and family in the United States, etc. The faith of many will be challenged as they experience increased persecutions, various trials, challenges and tribulations. Some Christians may waver or even question their faith. Some Christians will become weary and discouraged.

Regardless of what your personal situation is, God is aware of it and will fight for you. He fought for you before you were born and continues to do that for you even up to the present. Remember that the God who rules in the affairs of men, rules over circumstances that threaten your life, your dreams, and your destiny. He will never forsake you nor leave you!

Making it Personal

What one specific truth is God teaching me today?

....

....

....

....

One way to practically apply what God has taught me today...

....

....

....

....

*What do I want to tell God today concerning what
He taught me?* [**My Prayer**] ....

....

....

....

....

My Personal Declaration for Today [**Write it down
and speak it over and over**] ....

....

....

....

....

COUNTING YOUR BLESSINGS

Take this opportunity to reflect over what you have learned in your interaction with God this week. It will be helpful if you write down your experiences

1. Of the lessons or truths God taught you this week, write down which one ministered to you above all the others?

   ....

   ....

   ....

   ....

2. Mention one experience you had this week that made that particular lesson or truth more real to you than before?

   ....

   ....

   ....

   ....

3. What was the verse that you were able to memorize out of the verses presented for the week?

4. Reflect over the lessons for the week. Pray and make the following Prophetic Declarations for the coming week

I come boldly to the throne of grace through the blood of Jesus; I obtain exemption from judgement and enjoy divine grace to overcome all challenges in the name of Jesus.

I declare by divine authority, your word has preeminence over every stubborn problem in my life in the name of Jesus.

I establish your dominion over my life, family, community, Church and nation in the name of Jesus.

I declare peace over my life, family, church, community and nation in the name of Jesus.

Rule in my affairs O Lord and cause me to possess my possessions this year in the name of Jesus!

TIME IS IN GOD'S HANDS

Meditate on Psalm 31:14-15

Memorize Ecclesiastes 3:11-12

"He has made everything beautiful in its time. He has also set eternity in the human heart; yet no one can fathom what God has done from beginning to end."

Make it Real

The astronomers have studied much of space and the planets in the universe. Every day they come up with new discoveries. They have studied the movements of the planets to the point that they can predict the date and time when we are going to experience either the eclipse of the moon or the eclipse of the sun. We experience these with emotions of excitement and take pictures and talk about them.

One thing the astronomers have not been able to predict is what happens in the

101

history of mankind's life on earth. We are still struggling to determine when the earth began and for how long we have lived on earth. This is where our limitations must humbly submit to God's infinite knowledge. God does not think about time. What we call time is in His hands. God knows the end from the beginning. Even though He does not have a beginning or an end, we call Him Alpha and Omega, the Beginning and the End.

If you struggle with God's control over time, write this statement and place it in a visible location: "but when the fullness of the time was come... God" This is from Galatians 4:4.

I do not know what your age is, but I have heard people look at their age and think their lives are over because they have not been able to achieve much in life. Whatever your age, I invite you to think again in the light of the fact that time is in God's hands and He has absolute control over time, including your times on earth. God's timing is never too late.

Making it Personal

What one specific truth is God teaching me today? ....
....
....
....

One way to practically apply what God has taught me today...
....
....
....

What do I want to tell God today concerning what He taught me? [My Prayer] ....
....
....
....
....

My Personal Declaration for Today [Write it down and speak it over and over] ....
....
....
....
....

GOD'S TIMING IS THE BEST

Meditate on John 7:1-8

Memorize Psalm 75: 2

When the proper time has come [for executing My judgments], I will judge uprightly [says the Lord].

Make it Real

God made a prophetic declaration in Genesis 3:15, the fulfillment of which would bring liberty to mankind who at that time put himself under the bondage of the devil through disobedience. If you study your Bible well, you already know how long it took for this to happen. Several generations of God's people looked forward to the fulfillment of this prophecy; however, it was not yet time for the manifestation of this word.

Theological scholars can perfectly delineate the events that God allowed to happen in preparation for the coming of the Messiah.

These events were perfectly orchestrated so that humanity would not doubt and struggle to believe that Jesus was and is God's Savior for humanity.

You have to understand that when we speak of God's timing, we are not just talking about dates. It has nothing to do with calendar of activities. It has to do with the preparation which is necessary for God to set things in its proper place. Some of us might think there is a delay, however, God is using that time to lay the proper foundation. What needs to be put in place before that breakthrough child you are expecting arrives? What things must be in place before that million-dollar business materializes? What changes does God want to work out in your personal life before He promotes you into that prestigious position you so much desire? Sincerely, you cannot say you know the answers to any of these questions. The truth is that God knows best. Submit to God's timing and trust that He is working it out.

Making it Personal

What one specific truth is God teaching me today? ....
....
....
....

One way to practically apply what God has taught me today..
....
....
....

What do I want to tell God today concerning what He taught me? [My Prayer] ....
....
....
....
....

My Personal Declaration for Today [Write it down and speak it over and over] ....
....
....
....

WAITING ON GOD

Meditate on James 5:7-11

> **Memorize** Psalm 37:7
>
> *Be still before the LORD and wait patiently for him; do not fret when people succeed in their ways, when they carry out their wicked schemes.*

Make it Real

There is a lot we can learn from farmers. For every seed the farmer plants, there is a gestation period. The gestation period is the time it takes for your seed to germinate and grow. Gestation periods vary from plant to plant, usually shorter for simple plants like grains and vegetables. However, it would take longer for larger plants such as trees. Farmers know when to expect their harvest so they do not look for fruit until the gestation time has been completed. It is the same with women. Once a woman discovers that she is due to give birth, she knows that it will take at least 9 months for her seed to be born. No woman wants her child to come before the delivery due date otherwise there might be complications. There are extremely important developmental stages which are critical for the child to complete before it comes into the world.

In life, whenever you are expecting to bear fruit or any good thing to come to pass, there is always a waiting period. There are no short-cuts , no matter how anointed or gifted you are. Waiting becomes meaningful if God is the Object of your waiting. If you are waiting on an uncle, an aunty, your parents, or even your President to establish you in life, may the Lord have mercy on you. Reflect on your capacity to be patient and wait on God. How have you done so far ?

Making it Personal

What one specific truth is God teaching me today?..
....
....
....

One way to practically apply what God has taught me today...

....

....

....

What do I want to tell God today concerning what He taught me? [My Prayer].....................

....

....

....

....

My Personal Declaration for Today [Write it down and speak it over and over] ....

....

....

....

....

RIGHT PLACE AT RIGHT TIME

Meditate on 1 Samuel 17:32-37

Memorize Esther 4:14

"For if you remain silent at this time, relief and deliverance for the Jews will arise from another place, but you and your father's family will perish. And who knows but that you have come to your royal position for such a time as this?"

Make it Real

There was the sound of war, an atmosphere of fear and trembling, not the sound of guns and bullets and of the noise of detonating bombs, but the occasional rumblings of a single voice, reverberating through the camp of Israel. There was no life in any man.

Just then a shepherd boy walks on to the scene. His initial agenda was not to fight but to provide food to his brethren. In the same way that Joseph went to provide food to his brethren the day he was sold into slavery. This time the outcome was different, the shepherd boy was not sold into slavery. He was not even aware that his skills and courage would be needed at that particular moment. The king provided him a chance to speak and granted David his request to conquer this giant. In spite of his youth, the King had no other recourse. Desperate, he allowed David the opportunity to confront this giant who had been bullying the Israelites for some time.

I am sure David's parents had no clue their son was needed during that time; but God who knows the beginning from the end and who had a call upon David's life launched David into his destiny. David was confronted with a situation and his passion for God's glory was activated.

Is it possible that God has been positioning you for an appointed time and place? Find out what is being activated in you as you observe what is happening around you in your work place, your community, at church, within your family, with your friends and the like. Will you be ready for God's call on your life?

Making it Personal

What one specific truth is God teaching me today?...
....
....
....
....

One way to practically apply what God has taught me today...
....
....
....

What do I want to tell God today concerning what He taught me? [My Prayer].................
....
....
....
....

My Personal Declaration for Today [Write it down and speak it over and over] ....
....
....
....

QUICK TO SEE OPPORTUNITY

Meditate on 1 Corinthians 3:5-9

Memorize Ephesians 5:15-16

"Be very careful, then, how you live—not as unwise but as wise, making the most of every opportunity, because the days are evil."

Making it Real

The story is told of a shoe company that sent their staff to visit a newly developed community to investigate the prospects for establishing a shoe company in the same area. They came back and said that the prospects were poor. Over eighty per cent of the people were walking barefooted and were not complaining. The group stated, "They would not buy our shoes if we send them there, let alone establish a show manufacturing company". A second group from another company went to the same community and came back with a different story. Realizing that the people walked barefooted, they reasoned; "if only we teach the people the values and the beauty of wearing shoes, we have a great marketing opportunity". I am sure you can imagine which of the shoe manufacturing companies became successful.

This scenario describes two different attitudes that are very common in life. Many people can be pessimistic and see only one side of an issue – the challenging side or the one that potentially poses a lot of obstacles or difficulty. Sometimes the good things in life are contained in the most non-appealing packages. Today's passage shows that God provides opportunities to each one of us. We do not have to let our opportunity pass by because we are not able to see the larger picture or because we are not discerning properly. Think about those instances in your lifetime when you allowed a good opportunity to pass you by because you were not looking at the situation from the right perspective. What would you have done differently?

Making it Personal

What one specific truth is God teaching me today? ....
....
....
....
....

One way to practically apply what God has taught me today....................................
....
....
....

What do I want to tell God today concerning what He taught me? [My Prayer] ....
....
....
....

My Personal Declaration for Today [Write it down and speak it over and over] ....
....
....
....

CAPTURE OPPORTUNITY

Meditate on Matthew 13:44-46

Memorize Ecclesiastes 9:10

"Whatever your hand finds to do, do it with all your might, for in the realm of the dead, where you are going, there is neither working nor planning nor knowledge nor wisdom."

Make it Real

If God orders your footsteps and leads you to the right place at the right time and you find an opportunity that becomes the breakthrough you have been waiting for all your life, how do you respond? Read through our passage for today again. Jesus is telling us that in any opportunity we are provided that we must give it our all. We should not do anything half-heartedly. Selling all you have to buy a field that contains a treasure is not a haphazard process. It comes with a sacrifice. The only way someone would sell all he has to buy a property is because of the potential or value he sees in the property beyond what he's sold. These are windows of opportunities that God provides Himself and can be trusted.

Elsewhere, Jesus lamented over people giving all kinds of excuses for not being ready to follow Him. They probably did not have an understanding of who Jesus was nor did they come into the revelation of how the courses of their lives would dramatically change by following Jesus. These windows of opportunities do not come often, so when they do come we have to let go of whatever would hinder us, invest our time and energy into them, and reap the benefits that God has waiting us.

I would encourage you to evaluate every place where you have channeled your resources, your time and your energy. Analyze if what you are investing your time in are opportunities from God. It would be a tragedy for you to be involved in something that is not ordained by God. The price would be fruitless. Seek God's face in whatever you do and be sure that you are walking in His perfect will.

Making it Personal

What one specific truth is God teaching me today?..

One way to practically apply what God has taught me today..

What do I want to tell God today concerning what He taught me? [My Prayer] ....

My Personal Declaration for Today [Write it down and speak it over and over] ....

COUNTING YOUR BLESSINGS

Take this opportunity to reflect over what you have learned in your interaction with God this week. It will be helpful if you write down your experiences

1. Think about the lessons or truths that God revealed to you this week, which one ministered to you the most? ....

   ....

   ....

   ....

   ....

2. Mention one experience you had this week that made that particular lesson or truth more real to you than before?

   ....

   ....

   ....

   ....

   ....

3. What was the verse that you were able to memorize out of the verses presented for the week? ....
....
....
....
....

4. Reflect over the lessons for the week. Pray and make the following Prophetic Declarations for the coming week

I declare in the name of Jesus, that my times are in God's hands.

I believe that delays are not denials therefore my miracles will manifest in God's timing in the name of Jesus.

As I wait on God, I declare that every demonic orchestration by the enemy to divert my breakthrough is fiercely resisted in the name of Jesus.

Holy Ghost, open my eyes to see all the opportunities around me. I will not be denied my blessings in the name of Jesus.

I locate my blessings and I take them in the name of Jesus.

BE TRUSTWORTHY

Meditate on Judges 16:6-17

Memorize Colossians 3:9

"Do not lie to one another, seeing that you have put off the old self with its practices and have put on the new self, which is being renewed in knowledge after the image of its creator."

Make it Real

Today's passage presents us with a picture of betrayal and lack of trustworthiness. It is a story of insincerity breeding insincerity. Delilah wanted to know the secret of Sampson's strength; however, her motives were wrong. Samson knew that he was not supposed to disclose the secret of his strength and did not honor or obey God when he gave in to Delilah's request. He should have been honest and told Delilah that to do so would be in direct violation of God's request. Neither of them could trust one another. Both reaped the seeds of dishonesty- they died on the same day.

The absence of trustworthiness has permeated every fabric of our society. If this same lack of trust permeates the church, we will be in serious trouble. The church is the place where we are exhorted to be honest with each other, especially as Christians. Trouble starts when one party becomes untrustworthy. When trust is violated, it leaves the victim hurt and disillusioned. He/she feels that you can no longer be trusted and draws the same conclusion for the whole church. Let us deal honestly with one another and be worthy of the call that God has placed upon our lives—especially as representatives of Christ.

Making it Personal

What one specific truth is God teaching me today?...
....
....
....

One way to practically apply what God has taught me today.................................

....

....

....

....

What do I want to tell God today concerning what He taught me? [My Prayer]..................

....

....

....

....

My Personal Declaration for Today [Write it down and speak it over and over]...............

....

....

....

....

INTEGRITY

Meditate on Job 2:1-10

Memorize Psalms 15:1-2

"O LORD, who may abide in Your tent? Who may dwell on Your holy hill? He who walks with integrity, and works righteousness, and speaks truth in his heart."

Make it Real

Integrity has been generally accepted as the quality of being honest and having strong moral principles; moral uprightness. It is generally a personal choice to uphold oneself to consistent moral and ethical standards, the state of being whole and undivided.

As such, when we say someone has integrity, we mean that they act consistently according to the values, beliefs and principles they claim to hold. This is what is commonly expressed as "what you see is what you get". In business, think about integrity as buying a product and discovering that its characteristics are exactly as the ones mentioned in the advertisement on radio or TV.

Consider Job, and how God was able to vouch for his integrity. There was no doubt in God's mind, of where Job stood. Job did not waver in his faith in God and was not double-minded. If Job were living in our world today, all the media houses would be surrounding Job's house to interview him and have him on their front page.

I want you to meditate on the passage again and ask to what extent God can vouch for your integrity like He did for Job. In the quiet moments of your life, you can engage the Holy Spirit in this exercise; like David prayed and said, "search me O Lord and know my heart today..."

Making it Personal

What one specific truth is God teaching me today?

....

....

....

One way to practically apply what God has taught me today..

....

....

....

What do I want to tell God today concerning what He taught me? [**My Prayer**] ....

....

....

....

....

My Personal Declaration for Today [**Write it down and speak it over and over**] ....

....

....

....

....

SACRIFICE

Meditate on Isaiah 53:1-6

Memorize Hebrews 2:9

"But we do see Jesus, who was made lower than the angels for a little while, now crowned with glory and honor because he suffered death, so that by the grace of God he might taste death for everyone."

Make it Real

There are many individuals in society who made great sacrifices for humanity. One example from Africa's history is Stephen Bantu Biko of South Africa (1946–1977). Steve Biko, regarded as an icon in the anti-apartheid movement, founded several organizations in an effort to mobilize Black people against the racist apartheid regime in South Africa. Biko co-founded the South African Students' Organization in 1968, an all-Black student organization focusing on the resistance of apartheid. He later founded the Black Consciousness Movement (BCM), which would empower and mobilize much of the urban Black population, and co-founded the Black People's Convention in 1972.

Biko was arrested many times for his anti-apartheid activism. On Sept. 12, 1977, he died in police custody from injuries he sustained from the arresting officers. In 1997, five officers confessed to killing Biko after reportedly filling an application for amnesty to the Truth and Reconciliation Commission.

Although the things that Biko stood for were honorable and noble, we all know that the greatest sacrifice is that of Jesus standing in our place to receive the punishment for our sins so we can be saved. Most of the times we are not even called to physically die for others, yet we would not even sacrifice the smallest things on behalf of another.

That question to ask yourself is, what are you doing to emulate His example of self-sacrifice?

Making it Personal

What one specific truth is God teaching me today?

....

....

....

....

One way to practically apply what God has taught me today...

....

....

....

What do I want to tell God today concerning what He taught me? **[My Prayer]** ....

....

....

....

....

My Personal Declaration for Today **[Write it down and speak it over and over]** ....

....

....

....

....

BE RELIABLE

Meditate on Matthew 21:29-31

Memorize Isaiah 54:10

"For the mountains may be removed and the hills may shake, But My loving kindness will not be removed from you, And My covenant of peace will not be shaken," Says the LORD who has compassion on you."

Make it Real

Reflect again on the parable Jesus told in our passage for today. Consider if the two sons were your children, your siblings, your friends, your subordinates in an office, or even your partners in a business. Which one of them would you entrust things to be done, especially those things that are valuable to you? The answer is obvious.

We all want to be sure that the person we are asking to do something for us will surely do it. We all could probably relate to the experience of sending some material to the seamstress or tailor to make an outfit – an outfit you are expecting to wear in three weeks. The seamstress tells you the outfit will be ready in a week. Three days prior, you call and you are told that the material has been cut, but then you have receive a long list of reasons and excuses why your outfit may not be ready for the day you originally planned. Would you recommend your seamstress to someone else? She has not shown that she is reliable.

Our memory verse today establishes the reliability of God towards us. God is our Standard for reliability. Can God also rely on us for anything? Can God rely on you to tell the watchman in your community that Jesus loves him? Can God rely on you to show love to the needy around you? Can Jesus rely on you to visit the sick in your area who attends the same church with you? Can God rely on you to speak to a lost world about His unchanging truth? Start giving answers to this question in your devotion today.

Making it Personal

What one specific truth is God teaching me today?

....

....

....

....

One way to practically apply what God has taught me today..

....

....

....

*What do I want to tell God today concerning what He taught me? [**My Prayer**]* ....

....

....

....

....

*My Personal Declaration for Today [**Write it down and speak it over and over**]* ....

....

....

....

....

BEING TEACHABLE

Meditate on Amos 4:6-13

Memorize Psalm 32:8-9

"I will instruct you and teach you in the way you should go; I will counsel you with my loving eye on you. Do not be like the horse or the mule, which have no understanding but must be controlled by bit and bridle or they will not come to you."

Make it Real

Think back and recall a moment when your friend or child or spouse was not feeling well and the doctor prescribed medication for them. Even if you wanted to take the medicine on his/her behalf, there would be no value. How would your loved one get healed?

This same truth applies to the learning principle. You cannot study for someone else. You might be able to teach, provide the resources, and try to motivate the individual, however, they are responsible for absorbing the information and applying it. One of the major hindrances to learning is not the absence of learning material, or the absence of a facilitator of learning, or even the motivation. If an individual does not have a teachable spirit, he will not be receptive to learning anything. The person already thinks they know everything or at least has an answer for everything. A teachable spirit reflects an intentional desire to want to know. There is a willingness to hear a different perspective or to continue growing and learning. Without this teachable spirit, it is even difficult for God to teach these individuals because of their unwillingness to budge from their position.

God uses several means to teach us, either through different circumstances, or through others. If we continue to prove to be unteachable, in order to save us from His punishment, He may have to use a harsher method, for example, God had to humble Nebuchadnezzar and caused him to live in the woods for seven seasons to learn a simple truth that it is God who rules in the affairs of men. An unteachable spirit is a terrible trait.

Making it Personal

What one specific truth is God teaching me today?

....

....

....

....

One way to practically apply what God has taught me today...

....

....

....

*What do I want to tell God today concerning what He taught me? [**My Prayer**]* ....

....

....

....

....

*My Personal Declaration for Today [**Write it down and speak it over and over**]* ....

....

....

....

....

FIRM AND RESOLUTE

Meditate on Daniel 3:13-23

Memorize Philippians 1:27

"Only let your manner of life be worthy of the gospel of Christ, so that whether I come and see you or am absent, I may hear of you that you are standing firm in one spirit, with one mind striving side by side for the faith of the gospel."

Make it Real

Years back we read of stories about Richard Wurmbrand and his wife suffering in the former Soviet Union because they would not denounce their faith in Christ. Several of their testimonies were published in their book, "Tortured for Christ". Their stories are a continuation of the experience of Peter and the other disciples when they were beaten and charged to not speak again in the name of Jesus. This is impossible for a believer who truly knows and loves the Lord.

Earlier in biblical history, Daniel and the three Hebrew boys purposed in their hearts that they would not defile themselves. They were firm and resolute in their minds. The Apostle Paul in his writing to the Ephesians exhorts us to take a stand after having done all. Sometimes in life, you will have to take a stand for the convictions that God has given you no matter how unpopular.

Today, in several parts of the world, Christians are being threatened with all kinds of conditions just so that they will deny their faith in Christ. It appears in these last days when men are becoming lovers of pleasure more than lovers of God, the believer is going to face intense persecution in all forms. Let us not think of persecution only in terms of beatings and killings; one form of persecution already happening in America is scorn for the believer, name calling, stereotyping of believers, etc., the average Christian fears they will lose their American identity, and that is more important to them than being Christians. What accusations are you facing as a result of your stand for Jesus Christ?

Making it Personal

What one specific truth is God teaching me today?

....

....

....

....

One way to practically apply what God has taught me today...

....

....

....

*What do I want to tell God today concerning what He taught me? [**My Prayer**]*................................

....

....

....

....

*My Personal Declaration for Today [**Write it down and speak it over and over**]* ....

....

....

....

....

COUNTING YOUR BLESSINGS

> *Take this opportunity to reflect over what you have learned in your interaction with God this week. It will be helpful if you write down your experiences*

1. Think about the lessons or truths that God revealed to you this week, which one ministered to you the most? ....

   ....

   ....

   ....

   ....

2. Mention one experience you had this week that made that particular lesson or truth more real to you than before?

   ....

   ....

   ....

   ....

3. What was the verse that you were able to memorize out of the verses presented for the week? ....
....
....
....
....

4. Reflect over the lessons for the week. Pray and make the following Prophetic Declarations for the coming week

I declare in the name of Jesus, that as I stay focused on the word of God, the nature of Christ will be formed in me.

I will not be conformed to the world; I will be transformed by the renewing of my mind and I will prove through my life, that the will of God is good, acceptable and perfect.

I declare through the transforming power of the word of God that I will be trust worthy, I will walk in integrity and be reliable; I refuse to walk in disobedience, I will be teachable in the name of Jesus.

Teach me oh Lord, to live a life of sacrifice as you did by laying down your life for me. Enable me to serve faithfully in your church in the name of Jesus.

REALM OF NO LIMITS

Meditate on 1 Corinthians 2:1-9

Memorize Psalm 147:4-5

"He tells the number of the stars; he calls them all by their names. Great is our Lord, and of great power: his understanding is infinite."

Make it Real

It is often difficult for the human mind to think of the total absence of limits. In order to check in to see how your children are doing you have to go to their rooms. You have no idea what is happening outside until you step out of your home. You realize that as the sun rises and sets that your time is limited.

As you progress and age, you are constantly reminded of your own physical limitations. As humans, there are limits in terms of what we are able to do. Although this is the case for us, we must remember that God is not like us! God is all powerful, all knowing, and all seeing. Time and space are not limited to God. He lives in the realm of no limits. When Jesus came to earth, he was confronted with some of our limitations for example it took him a few days to get to Lazarus although he knew that Lazarus was sick and dying.

Read today's passage again. Can you realize a world much, much bigger than what we can think of? The Apostle Paul talks about what no eye has seen, nor has any ear heard, etc. The amount of what we can know is endless. Elsewhere Jesus told His disciples there is so much He wanted to teach them. Jesus' death and resurrection made it easier for us to respond to God's invitation into the no limits realm but we struggle every day. In the no limits realm we see as God sees and therefore will act as He would in our situations on earth.

Making it Personal

What one specific truth is God teaching me today?

....

....

....

....

One way to practically apply what God has taught me today ....

....

....

....

What do I want to tell God today concerning what He taught me? [**My Prayer**] ....

....

....

....

....

My Personal Declaration for Today [**Write it down and speak it over and over**] ....

....

....

....

....

GOD KNOWS NO LIMITS

Meditate on 1 Tim 6:13-16

Memorize 1 Kings 8:27

"But will God indeed dwell on the earth? Behold, heaven and the highest heaven cannot contain You, how much less this house which I have built!

Make it Real

Unfortunately, one of the biggest mistakes that humanity makes is placing boundaries on what God can do. We try to conceptualize who God is by our limited human understanding and it is just not possible. We can try to imagine how infinite and vast his wisdom is by the minute accomplishments that man has done in the field of science and technology, however, even with all of the intelligence and knowledge of man combined—it is not enough to define who God is! Just when you think you might have God figured out, there may be a situation or a circumstance that makes you wonder why God allows certain things to happen or why he uses certain individuals to help advance His divine purposes or will.

Awesome has been a common word used to describe who God is. However, today the word awesome has become a commonly used word and unfortunately loses its potency when we use it to describe Him. Meditate on today's passage. Let us appreciate that we cannot wrap our limited minds around the awesomeness of God's glory. Remember not to place God in a box or dictate what He is capable of doing but do bask in the gloriousness of who He is- the great I AM.

Making it Personal

What one specific truth is God teaching me today?

....

....

....

....

One way to practically apply what God has taught me today ....

....

....

....

....

What do I want to tell God today concerning what He taught me? [**My Prayer**] ....

....

....

....

....

My Personal Declaration for Today [**Write it down and speak it over and over**] ....

....

....

....

....

REMOVE THE LIMITS

Meditate on John 16:7-16

Memorize 1 Corinthians 2:14

"The person without the Spirit does not accept the things that come from the Spirit of God but considers them foolishness, and cannot understand them because they are discerned only through the Spirit."

Make it Real

To be able to effectively progress in your relationship with a God who is limitless and awesome, you must first move out of the limitations of your human mind that is predominantly controlled by your brain and its functions. God is too big to be limited to our human thinking so this is why it is important to switch gears-so-to-speak when we are relating with Him. We do this by switching from our tendency to reason or rationalize to a faith-based mindset—this can only stem from the Holy Spirit.

What message is Jesus trying to give His disciples in today's passage? Does Jesus tell them how to shift gears? Yes, He does! He lamented over their inability to understand things in their current mindset, He knew that it would take revelation from the Holy Spirit who would teach them all things.

God knew we could not grasp the vastness of who He was by using our minds which had already been corrupted by sin in the Garden of Eden. This is the reason He made provision so that we could experience in the flesh. If you find yourself challenging God's unmistakable Glory and His word , it is clear that you have an unrenewed mind; you are still set in your old ways. When you consistently question the boundaries, exhortations, and instructions which God has graciously provided us in His word, remember this is exactly how it began in the Garden of Eden.

Warning: Do not be fooled by the inventions of man through the development of the human mind. God is not against the evolvement of mankind as long as it helps men discover how great God is!

Making it Personal

What one specific truth is God teaching me today?

....

....

....

....

One way to practically apply what God has taught me today ....

....

....

....

What do I want to tell God today concerning what He taught me? [**My Prayer**] ....

....

....

....

My Personal Declaration for Today [**Write it down and speak it over and over**] ....

....

....

....

....

LOOK BEYOND YOURSELF

Meditate on Psalm 121:1-8

Memorize John 15:5

"I am the vine; you are the branches. If you remain in me and I in you, you will bear much fruit; apart from me you can do nothing."

Make it Real

This Psalm starts with an interesting introduction: "I will lift up my eyes unto the hills, from where comes my help?" One would think the Psalmist is literally expecting help from the mountains. Just then he points us to the One who resides way beyond the hills and shows us that his help comes from Him.

The psalmist does not just leave us there. He goes on to help us understand his choice, and justifies his decision – all based on his knowledge of Him who resides beyond the hills. Note the characteristics of God which he lists, for which he is not ashamed to boast about. He places all of His trust in the infinite goodness of God. It is clear that the Psalmist is implying that we should do the same when we find ourselves in difficult situations. God made the heavens and the earth and all that is in it, but He we should not place our help in the things He created. Our help still resides in Him who made us in His image.

While we ponder over the Psalmists exhortation, Jesus makes it plain to us in His conversation with the disciples. Our prayers are never in vain; apart from God we can do nothing. However, when we abide in Jesus this gives us power to every prayer we make to our heavenly Father. In all things we have to look up to our Heavenly Father and abide in the Vine. This is the formula to experience victory and success in this life. When you search within yourself, you will clearly see your limitations; when you look to the Lord, you see things exactly the way He sees them. That is when impossible situations become possible. Where have you been looking for help all of these years?

Making it Personal

What one specific truth is God teaching me today?

....

....

....

....

One way to practically apply what God has taught me today ....

....

....

....

....

*What do I want to tell God today concerning what He taught me? [**My Prayer**]* ....

....

....

....

*My Personal Declaration for Today [**Write it down and speak it over and over**]* ....

....

....

....

....

BREAK OUT OF SATAN'S EMBALMENT

Meditate on John 11:38-44

Memorize Psalm 124:7-8

"We have escaped like a bird from the fowler's snare; the snare has been broken, and we have escaped. Our help is in the name of the LORD, the Maker of heaven and earth."

Make it Real

The Egyptians are very well known for the way they preserved the dead bodies of their dead kings and important people-mummification. After the person passed away, the body went through a preservation treatment prior to burial. This was done to prevent decay. With the help of the embalmers preserving the body, the say the soul would be able to recognize its own body. After burial, it becomes very difficult for tomb-raiders to break up the tomb, destroy the body and steal anything.

Think of Lazarus' preparation for burial in a similar way. He was bound with grave clothes all over. When Jesus called him to come forth from the grave, they still had to loose him from all of the bondage before he could get out. Likewise, many have been bound by the devil and need to be set from to come out of darkness.

I do not know how long you have been kept in bondage, however, – when the Lord of life visits you and commands you to come forth then you will be set free from the bondage of Satan. With help from the Maker of heaven and earth, you are the only one who knows the chains the devil has kept you in. I declare to you today that Jesus has set you free, remove the grave clothes yourself and come out alive again!

Making it Personal

What one specific truth is God teaching me today?

....

....

....

....

....

One way to practically apply what God has taught me today ....
....
....
....
....

What do I want to tell God today concerning what He taught me? [**My Prayer**] ....
....
....
....
....

My Personal Declaration for Today [**Write it down and speak it over and over**] ....
....
....
....
....

FIRE AT FULL CAPACITY

Meditate on Proverbs 6:6-11

Memorize Colossians 3:23-24

"Whatever you do, work heartily, as for the Lord and not for men, knowing that from the Lord you will receive the inheritance as your reward."

Make it Real

Capacity is the amount your manufacturing operation has the ability to produce. A publication in the International News dated Tuesday, December 31, 2013, reported: The Lahore Chamber of Commerce and Industry (LCCI) said that Pakistani abattoirs are working below capacity and the government should instead focus on improving their operations.

When companies are not meeting their financial goals, they have to make decisions on how to recoup their losses. Sometimes, employers will downsize the number of their employees and conduct a re-organization. Sometimes, they will increase the costs of their products. There are several variables which may cause organizations or people to perform at low capacity. Today's passage is discussing one of the possible factors.

Meditate again on the lessons God wants us to learn from one of His tiniest creatures on earth. Have you ever tried comparing yourself to this little animal? The ant is known for how diligently it is able to work. Many of us, like the ant, need to up our game and perform at full capacity.

If you can evangelize and win five souls a week, go ahead and do it. If you are a pastor with resources enough to engage a program that will lead to the growth and development of your members, do not be satisfied by a few complimentary comments here and there when you know you are performing below capacity. If you are running your business capable of producing 1000 units of your product, never accept 800 as a job well done. Think of different areas of your life where you know you can do much better. Do it as unto the Lord!

Making it Personal

What one specific truth is God teaching me today?

....

....

....

....

One way to practically apply what God has taught me today ....

....

....

....

What do I want to tell God today concerning what He taught me? [**My Prayer**] ....

....

....

....

....

My Personal Declaration for Today [**Write it down and speak it over and over**] ....

....

....

....

....

COUNTING YOUR BLESSINGS

Take this opportunity to reflect over what you have learned in your interaction with God this week. It will be helpful if you write down your experiences

1. Think about the lessons or truths that God revealed to you this week, which one ministered to you the most? ....

   ....

   ....

   ....

   ....

2. Mention one experience you had this week that made that particular lesson or truth more real to you than before?

   ....

   ....

   ....

   ....

   ....

3. What was the verse that you were able to memorize out of the verses presented for the week?..
....
....
....

4. Reflect over the lessons for the week. Pray and make the following Prophetic Declarations for the coming week

By faith I enter into the realm of no limitation in the name of Jesus; I know my God is able to do exceedingly abundantly above all that I ask or even imagine.

I declare by divine authority, all forms of demonic limitations placed over my life, family and finances in the realms of the spirit are broken in the name of Jesus.

I look beyond myself to the God of my salvation; by His power I break out of every demonic embalmment and stagnation in the name of Jesus.

I move from the valley to the mountain top and I operate through the power of the Holy Ghost at full capacity by divine authority in the name of Jesus.

THE MIND, THE BATTLEFIELD

Meditate on 2 Corinthians 10:1-6

Memorize 2 Corinthians 4:3-4

"And even if our gospel is veiled, it is veiled to those who are perishing. The god of this age has blinded the minds of unbelievers, so that they cannot see the light of the gospel that displays the glory of Christ, who is the image of God."

Make it Real

As humans we process a lot of information through our minds. The raw mind is a gateway that cannot select what enters. What makes the human mind a battlefield is that the mind has the capacity to receive information from the spirit of God through our human spirit. At the same time evil spirits feed the mind, working through Satan's agencies in fallen humanity – the lust of the flesh, the lust of the eyes, and the pride of life.

161

You may not be aware that every day you are deciding to do what Satan is asking you to do or what God is asking you to do. The Christian who is aware of this ongoing battle takes time to process information that drops into the mind. He or she knows that information has to be discerned to determine whether or not it is contrary to Scripture.

Once you draw your conclusion, the outcome will lead to a mindset or a decision.

The mature mind will know which thoughts to dismiss and which thoughts are from the Lord. Someone once said you could not prevent birds from landing on your head while relaxing under a tree, but you could certainly prevent them from building nests in your hair. Use the Word of God to filter the information that you receive every day. The battle we face from day to day is in our mind. Unfortunately, none of us are free from this battle. Uproot the seeds that God did not plant, and sow the Word of God into your life and you will see the good fruit!

Making it Personal

What one specific truth is God teaching me today?

....

....

....

....

One way to practically apply what God has taught me today..

....

....

....

What do I want to tell God today concerning what He taught me? [**My Prayer**]..

....

....

....

My Personal Declaration for Today [**Write it down and speak it over and over**] ....

....

....

....

....

YOUR THOUGHTS DEFINE YOU

Meditate on Romans 12:1-3

Memorize Luke 6:45

"The good man out of the good treasure of his heart brings forth what is good; and the evil man out of the evil treasure brings forth what is evil; for his mouth speaks from that which fills his heart."

Make it Real

With the understanding of the mind as the battlefield, we understand the importance of how the mind functions. Knowing that the mind is a battlefield, we can surmise the importance of understanding the way that we think. The way we think has a direct impact on the decisions or choices we make from day-to-day. We can infer or make correlations on someone's thoughts by noting his or her behavior. The Word of God even states you will know them by their fruits.

Those who think God does not exist live their lives according to this belief. Some who believe that God is not relevant today do not want God to be used as the reference point in discussing what is right or wrong. A man's thoughts on marriage shows in how he treats his spouse and vice versa. Pastors treat their congregation members in accordance with what they think of them, and congregation members relate to their pastors by what they think of them.

We can definitely assume that man's thoughts have impact on his/her behavior. There are several facts about the mind that scholars refer to which the bible has already addressed - "As a man thinks in his heart, so is he". You are defined by the way you think in your heart.

This is the way the Word of God states that we should be "transformed by the renewal of the mind..." This means that there are strongholds in our thinking or mindset which need to be broken. No one can experience true change if he does not change his thinking pattern. The only way to do this is to meditate on God's Word. Spend some time today and make a list of thoughts or mindsets you felt led by the Holy Spirit to change.

Making it Personal

What one specific truth is God teaching me tod ay?..
....
....
....

One way to practically apply what God has taught me today...
....
....
....

*What do I want to tell God today concerning what He taught me? [**My Prayer**]* ....
....
....
....

*My Personal Declaration for Today [**Write it down and speak it over and over**]*..............................
....
....
....

PUT ON THE MIND OF CHRIST

Meditate on Philippians 2:1-11

Memorize 1 Corinthians 14:20

"Brothers and sisters, stop thinking like children. In regard to evil be infants, but in your thinking be adults."

Make it Real

The Apostle Paul in our passage today is addressing a very important issue that can be extended to other areas of our lives. Many of us have difficulty relating to people because of what we think about ourselves, and secondly what we think about other people. In African culture, there are individuals who belong to tribes who will never marry someone from a different tribe. This is because of a certain mindset that has already been developed about the other person's tribe. It is not uncommon to stereotype groups of people as inferior or superior based on superficial reasoning such as race, culture, nationality, or social standing.

Apostle Paul is exhorting us to think soberly about ourselves so that we do not misjudge others before we get to know them. People who have achieved celebrity status or have social status because of family legacy in their country in certain instances tend to think more highly of themselves in comparison to others.

Remember that whatever name you bear, whatever your background is, whatever men say to you about yourself, whatever lofty views which you have about yourself, do not be tempted to meditate on those thoughts and let them negatively impact your relationship with other people. Meditate through our passage today and let the Holy Spirit minister to you. Your life will truly never be the same again.

Making it Personal

What one specific truth is God teaching me today?

....

....

....

....

One way to practically apply what God has taught
me today...

....

....

....

What do I want to tell God today concerning what He
taught me? [*My Prayer*]..

....

....

....

My Personal Declaration for Today [**Write it
down and speak it over and over**] ....

....

....

....

....

FEED YOUR MIND RIGHT

Meditate on Romans 8:5-7

Memorize

"Keep this Book of the Law always on your lips; meditate on it day and night, so that you may be careful to do everything written in it. Then you will be prosperous and successful."

Make it Real

There is a lot that we can learn from farmers. They plants seeds in the soil and watch the seeds germinate. From the time of germination through harvest time, the farmer has the responsibility of making sure that the plant is properly growing through each stage of development through maturity. Through research, Agriculturists have discovered the specific kinds of nutrients necessary to fertilize and help the plants grow at each critical stage, including the right quantities. Whether it is natural or artificial fertilizers or a mixture of both, these are religiously provided according to the prescribed instruction to ensure plant growth.

The mind is like fertile ground. The thoughts that enter are like seeds. Like the farmer, we have the responsibility of providing nutrients to ensure that our mind will grow. We also have to uproot seeds that would grow into weeds.

So when we think about the seasons of life in which we find ourselves in, we have to ensure that we are feeding our minds with the right seeds.

So, what have you been feeding your mind on lately? Are they aligned with the word of God? Sort that out in today's devotion

Making it Personal

What one specific truth is God teaching me today?

....

....

....

....

One way to practically apply what God has taught me today..

....

....

....

*What do I want to tell God today concerning what He taught me? [**My Prayer**]*..

....

....

....

*My Personal Declaration for Today [**Write it down and speak it over and over**]* ....

....

....

....

....

INFORMED BY THE SPIRIT

Meditate on John 16:7-11

Memorize 2 Corinthians 4:11

"For who knows a person's thoughts except their own spirit within them? In the same way no one knows the thoughts of God except the Spirit of God."

Make it Real

If a young student wants to become a great scientist one day, the best thing for this student to do is shadow another scientist. This person would serve as a mentor or instructor to this young aspiring person. A great wealth of information, which is critical for the success of the student, would be passed on from the scientist.

This same principle applies to the development of one's spiritual life. The Christian life is not just simply obeying a set of rules and regulations; it is means taking on the characteristics of Christ. A relationship with Christ is critical for the growth of the believer. If there is no relationship, there can be no fruitful Christian life.

A lot of people struggle with their Christian life simply because they do not have a true and meaningful relationship with Christ. They may have started with a confession of faith, however, you need more than just a confession of faith to mature in your relationship with Christ. Even if your name if written in the Book of Life, you will spend time in the word to grow.

God knew that the people who would develop a true relationship with Christ were the people who had a revelation of who Christ was and understood the real significance of what Christ did for us on the cross. This is not about having book knowledge of Christ, it's about experiencing His love and mercy and rejoicing in salvation. Take some time and think about your current relationship with Christ, are you experiencing the manifestation of His presence in your life? Do people see the evidence of Christ in you?

Making it Personal

What one specific truth is God teaching me today?

....

....

....

....

One way to practically apply what God has taught me today...

....

....

....

*What do I want to tell God today concerning what He taught me? [**My Prayer**]...*

....

....

....

*My Personal Declaration for Today [**Write it down and speak it over and over**]* ....

....

....

....

....

WHATEVER IS PURE

Meditate on Philippians 4:8-9

Memorize Colossians 3:1-2

"Since, then, you have been raised with Christ, set your hearts on things above, where Christ is, seated at the right hand of God. Set your minds on things above, not on earthly things."

Make it Real

Do you know that there is a direct relationship with what you feed your mind and what you want to become? When you became a Christian, you repented of your sins and Christ made you a new person. You wanted Jesus to make you like Him. Here is the truth; Jesus is a pure and holy person and that is exactly what He wants to make you. He wants you to become so pure and holy that the people who knew you before you met Jesus will see the difference and know that Jesus really did something special in your life.

176

Purity and holiness begins with your mind. This is what we have been meditating on this whole week. The Holy Spirit is feeding you with knowledge of Jesus Christ. He is the only person who can do that. You also have a responsibility to be careful what you feed your mind. This is one area many Christians still struggle with. Too many people Christians are consciously or unconsciously feeding their minds with things that make it difficult for their minds to develop the purity they desire. As a Christian, you have to learn to filter through all the information that will come your way on a daily basis. There is a lot of information in the media today that is simply not edifying – magazines, books, the Internet, movies, adverts, etc. most of the information from these avenues are full of information that promote sensual, immoral thinking, and behavior that is nowhere close to the person you want to become. Guard yourself from the things of the world, and make sure your feed yourself with the things of the Spirit and see how God can transform your life!

Making it Personal

*What one specific truth is God teaching me tod
ay?*...
....
....
....

*One way to practically apply what God has taught
me today*..
....
....
....

*What do I want to tell God today concerning what He
taught me? [**My Prayer**]*...
....
....
....

*My Personal Declaration for Today [**Write it down
and speak it over and over**]*.......................................
....
....
....

COUNTING YOUR BLESSINGS

Take this opportunity to reflect over what you have learned in your interaction with God this week. It will be helpful if you write down your experiences

1. Think about the lessons or truths that God revealed to you this week, which one ministered to you the most? ....

   ....

   ....

   ....

   ....

2. Mention one experience you had this week that made that particular lesson or truth more real to you than before?

   ....

   ....

   ....

   ....

3. What was the verse that you were able to memorize out of the verses presented for the week?..
....
....
....

4. Reflect over the lessons for the week. Pray and make the following Prophetic Declarations for the coming week

I declare in the name of Jesus, I live in the realm of no limits because my Heavenly Father has no limits. I break out of all forms of limitations placed over my life by messengers of Satan in the name of Jesus. I rise above soulish prayers by carnal Christians and darts thrown against me by wicked personalities in the name of Jesus. I break out of every confinement in the name of Jesus.

I look beyond myself to the realm of God, where all forms of limitations over my life have been removed. I declare by divine authority, I operate at full capacity by the help of God and I declare in the name of Jesus my enemies will not comprehend the extent of my elevation in the name of Jesus.

KEEP YOUR MIND STAYED ON GOD

Meditate on Romans 1:28-31

> **Memorize** Isaiah 26:3
>
> *"Thou wilt keep him in perfect peace, whose mind is stayed on thee: because he trusteth in thee."*

Making it Real

In almost every court of law in the United States today it is unconstitutional to have the Ten Commandments posted anywhere. This is interesting as those same law courts are trying people on a regular basis for all kinds of crimes – theft [thou shall not steal], murder [thou shall not kill] character assassinations [thou shall not bear false witness], etc. Although contradictory, the law charges people who steal, and commit murders, however, the very foundation of what God tried to establish many generations ago has been rejected to appease people.

This simply represents man's intention to remove God out of his life. Unfortunately, this is a reflection of the enemy's attempt to undermine God's authority. Unfortunately, many Americans have spoken. They do not think there is a place for God in America-- starting with their homes, and schools, etc. The scriptures are clear on what happens to people who reject God and His Wisdom.

Does it look strange that there is untold hardship in countries that have turned their backs on God? There is only one explanation – the peace that comes with retaining God in the minds of the people just goes away. If the people or their countries experience some peace, it is most probably because there are some people who retain God in their minds. For their sake, total destruction is upheld. How much of the thoughts of God occupy your thinking in a 24-hour day for seven days a week?

Making it Personal

What one specific truth is God teaching me tod ay? ....
....
....

....

One way to practically apply what God has taught me today...
....
....
....

What do I want to tell God today concerning what He taught me? [***My Prayer***]...
....
....
....

My Personal Declaration for Today [***Write it down and speak it over and over***] ....
....
....
....
....

BE ON THE ALERT

Meditate on: Matthew 13:24-30

Memorize 1 Peter 5:8

Be sober, be vigilant; because your adversary the devil, as a roaring lion, walketh about, seeking whom he may devour:

Make it Real

Can you imagine what residents would do if it is announced that some thieves have entered a neighborhood? Your guess is as good as mine. Everyone would be alert because no one can be sure which house they will attack next. Where there is a neighborhood watch group, they would be alert; they would sit throughout the whole night and patrol within the community to make sure that the thieves do not have their way.

Being alert against the possible onslaught of thieves certainly influences our behavior. We protect the entrances to our houses with burglar proof, and make sure our doors and windows are always shut. When we go out, we come home early and secure our residences before we go to bed. We make sure we have direct lines to security companies, in case of any emergencies.

Can we practice the same alertness in our spiritual and moral lives? The Bible constantly warns us of our enemy the devil, whose goal is to take us out if he can. I say if he can because for the believer, God our heavenly Father fights on our behalf. Even then, if we lose guard, the devil takes advantage to make a mess of our lives.

I want you to do a bit of reflection. What have you done in the past 14 days to show that you are alert, watching to deal with the enemy you cannot see? The thieves and robbers do not come to your area every day; but be assured that the devil follows you everywhere you go. Is it that not enough reason for you to be alert as a Christian?

Making it Personal

What one specific truth is God teaching me today?

....

....
....
....

One way to practically apply what God has taught me today..
....
....
....

What do I want to tell God today concerning what He taught me? [**My Prayer**]..
....
....
....

My Personal Declaration for Today [**Write it down and speak it over and over**] ....
....
....
....
....

OVERCOMING TEMPTATION

Meditate on Genesis 4:1-8

Memorize 1 Corinthians 10:13

There hath no temptation taken you but such as is common to man: but God is faithful, who will not suffer you to be tempted above that ye are able; but will with the temptation also make a way to escape, that ye may be able to bear it.

Make it Real

How often have you heard people say when they are caught in the wrong, "the devil made me do it?" Many people blame the devil for the sins they commit. As Christians we know that the devil is always at our heels.

Although the devil will not stop coming to our gates, his intended victory over us is never guaranteed. It is our victory over him that is totally guaranteed. When the devil comes against us, in actual fact, he has come against Christ our Lord and Saviour. Together with Christ Jesus, we are greater than the devil and a thousand of his demons. We are already on the side of victory and all that is required of us is to stand and resist him in Jesus' name.

The Apostle Paul makes us understand that no temptation is greater than we can handle. God knows the temptation before it approaches your gates, and He knows that you are well able to overcome it. In fact, He always provides a way of escape in all such situations.

I want you to reflect on those temptations that you could not overcome; the situations in which you knew you had sinned. Carefully recollect if there was something you could have done differently that you ignored. Is it that you needed to run away from a particular situation but you did not? Is it that you could have prevented a situation from getting to an uncontrollable stage and you ignored the warnings?

A common example given is that, a young boy and girl or even a man and woman who are not married should avoid being alone in a room for a long time. Now reflect and evaluate your own behavior when you faced situations that were clearly temptations. How did you fare?

Making it Personal

What one specific truth is God teaching me today?

....

....

....

....

One way to practically apply what God has taught me today..

....

....

....

What do I want to tell God today concerning what He taught me? [***My Prayer***] ....

....

....

....

My Personal Declaration for Today [***Write it down and speak it over and over***] ....

....

....

....

TRIUMPHING IN TRIALS

Meditate on Job 1:6-12

Memorize 2 Corinthians 2:14

Now thanks be unto God, which always causeth us to triumph in Christ, and maketh manifest the savour of his knowledge by us in every place.

Make it Real

To triumph is to be victorious. Triumph also means to succeed, conquer and achieve something. A trial is like a test you go through. The examinations you write in school are meant to bring out the good in you. No one knows what is deep inside you. Your teacher has taught you a whole semester. You have diligently studied through thick and thin. The test is to prove to the whole world that you indeed have been studying the whole semester. Most students do not see testing time that way.

To many students, exam time is torture and they are gripped with fear and anxiety as exams approach. This scenario usually describes the student who has not studied at all. Students who were truly diligent hardly panic when the exam time-table is posted.

This same scenario presents us with two categories of Christians. First, those who have diligently walked with the Lord and learnt from Him and are daily becoming more and more like Jesus. Then there is the other category that has taken their Christian life rather casually. Can you tell which of them will experience triumph in the midst of trials? Can you tell which category will shake, fear and complain when trials knock at their door?

When Job went through trials, it was to prove his stature. It was not to show his weakness; it was to show his strengths. God said there was no one who feared Him like Job, and that is not a weakness. Job's trial started not as a result of living to satisfy the works of his flesh, but came about as a result of his commitment to God and His word. Trials often reveal our true state as believers. Are you going through trials? Be strong, God may be making his boast in you!

Making it Personal

What one specific truth is God teaching me today?
....
....
....
....

One way to practically apply what God has taught me today..
....
....
....

What do I want to tell God today concerning what He taught me? [**My Prayer**]..
....
....
....

My Personal Declaration for Today [**Write it down and speak it over and over**] ....
....
....
....
....

CHEERFUL IN TRIBULATIONS

Meditate on Acts 5:35-42

Memorize John 16:33

These things I have spoken unto you, that in me ye might have peace. In the world ye shall have tribulation: but be of good cheer; I have overcome the world.

Make it Real

Every day we hear news of Christians being persecuted in certain parts of the world, particularly in Muslim countries. We usually hold hands and pray for them. Sometimes we pray that the persecution will stop so they can worship God freely like we do in our countries. Other times, we pray that God should strengthen them so they can endure whatever hardships they are going through. Both are appropriate.

There is one prayer that is always right on target; it is that they should not get discouraged and that the peace of God should abide in their hearts in those situations. That prayer seems to be in line with Jesus' exhortation to His followers. He said in this world they would have tribulations but they should be of good cheer.

I believe we would help ourselves if we programmed our minds to think that we live in a world that is hostile to our God and His commandments. The Christian faith has often come under more pressure than any other faith in the entire world. The world cannot handle the gospel of salvation through the death and shed blood of Jesus Christ. That is the whole point of reference for the suffering true Christians go through.

Knowing that, Jesus showed us the way to stand up against persecution. He said we should be of good cheer. Any time Jesus asks us to do something, it means He knows we can. He actually strengthens us through the Holy Spirit to be able to do what He asks us to do.

Please go back to our passage for today and meditate on the disciples' attitude after they had been flogged.

Making it Personal

What one specific truth is God teaching me today?
....
....
....
....

One way to practically apply what God has taught me today..
....
....
....

What do I want to tell God today concerning what He taught me? **[My Prayer]**...
....
....
....

My Personal Declaration for Today **[Write it down and speak it over and over]**...........
....
....
....
....

DECLARE YOUR VICTORIES IN CHRIST

Meditate on Exodus 15:1-12

Memorize 1 Chronicles 29:11

"Yours, O LORD, is the greatness and the power and the glory and the victory and the majesty, indeed everything that is in the heavens and the earth; Yours is the dominion, O LORD, and You exalt Yourself as head over all.

Make it Real

Sometimes it is amazing that we are at a loss for words when we have to praise or worship God. We use phrases like "I praise You" and "I sing to You", and "I appreciate You". This sometimes creates the impression we have no victories to declare. As a child of God who is truly walking very close with the Lord on a daily basis, you always have some victory to declare. You always have a testimony. Sometimes it is important to be specific and thank God for all His benefits. Remember to count your blessings and praise God for the specific benefits you have received from Him just like the lone leper in the bible who came to thank Jesus for his healing when nine others went away taking their healing for granted.

Read our passage for today again and listen to Miriam and the women of Israel very well. They will teach you what it means to declare your victories. If someone comes to you and says that if God had not intervened, he would not have come to work alive, that is a declaration of the goodness of God.

Make a descriptive list of the victories you have won in the Lord in the past week. Read the statements out loud to yourself. Now read them prayerfully to the Lord in deep appreciation. When you go out and meet your friends anywhere – at work, at the beach, or wherever you find yourself, speak those statements aloud to them. That is declaring your victories. They will hear those declarations and also declare, "Truly God is good!"

Making it Personal

What one specific truth is God teaching me today?

....

....

....

....

One way to practically apply what God has taught me today..

....

....

....

What do I want to tell God today concerning what He taught me? [**My Prayer**]..

....

....

....

My Personal Declaration for Today [**Write it down and speak it over and over**].......................................

....

....

....

COUNTING YOUR BLESSINGS

Take this opportunity to reflect over what you have learned in your interaction with God this week. It will be helpful if you write down your experiences

1. Of the lessons or truths God taught you this week, write down which one ministered to you above all the others? ....

....

....

....

2. Mention one experience you had this week that made that particular lesson or truth more real to you than before?

....

....

....

3. What was the verse that you were able to memorize out of the verses presented for

the week?...
....
....

4. Reflect over the lessons for the week. Pray and make the following Prophetic Declarations for the coming week

Holy Spirit, I give you praise for who you are and for what you mean to me. You are the ever living God, full of grace and glory. I worship you in the beauty of your holiness; you are worthy to receive glory and honor.

I thank you for the promptings of your Spirit that helps me to stay watchful; causing me to escape the snares and traps of the enemy. I resist and overcome all manner of temptations in the name of Jesus.

I refuse to be depressed because of all the trials I am facing in the name of Jesus. I exchange every spirit of heaviness with the garment of praise.

Thanks be to God who always causes us to triumph in Christ and through us diffuses the fragrance of His knowledge in every place. Blessed be your mighty name forevermore. Amen

PERSEVERANCE

Meditate on 2 Timothy 4:1-5

Memorize Hebrews 10:39

But we are not of them who draw back unto perdition; but of them that believe to the saving of the soul.

Make it Real

Have you ever had a chat with an athlete? I am not talking about the sprinters; I mean the long-distance runners – the marathon, steeplechase and 5,000 meters runners. If you are interested in sports, you may even have had several opportunities to watch them engage in their races. That is a good object lesson for understanding perseverance.

You can see their faces each time the cameras focuses on them – sweat, squeezed faces, signs of aching bodies, you name them. These have every reason in the world to say, "I quit". They never quit however. They run till they cross the finishing line.

The Apostle Paul likens the Christian race to an athletic tournament. Our finishing line is the coming of our Lord Jesus Christ or the day God calls us home; whichever comes first. Until that time, there is nothing like quitting. Paul says for Christ's sake we are killed all day long. We are counted as sheep for the slaughter. In today's world, people persecute Christians and think they are right to do so.

In any race, only those who persevere to the end of the race are rewarded. Those who quit are disqualified. Paul was well aware of what lay ahead of Timothy which explains why he wrote to him the passage for today. How real today are some of the things Paul warned Timothy about? What will happen to the Christian if he does not persevere in his faith in the light of all that is going on today?

Making it Personal

What one specific truth is God teaching me tod ay? ....
....
....
....

One way to practically apply what God has taught me today...
....
....
....

What do I want to tell God today concerning what He taught me? **[My Prayer]**...
....
....
....

My Personal Declaration for Today **[Write it down and speak it over and over]**......................................
....
....
....

MARCH THROUGH A TROOP

Meditate on 2 Samuel 23:13-17

Memorize 2 Samuel 22:29-31

For thou art my lamp, O LORD: and the LORD will lighten my darkness.

For by thee I have run through a troop: by my God have I leaped over a wall.

As for God, his way is perfect; the word of the LORD is tried: he is a buckler to all them that trust in him.

Make it Real

Ponder over the following scenario. A little boy tried using a knife to cut through a piece of butter that had been moderately frozen. As he struggled, his friend told him to heat up the metal portion of the knife. It worked. The heat of the knife enabled it cut through the semi-frozen butter with such ease to their amazement.

Now think about going through a troop made up of strong men armed in battle; like we read in today's passage. Can you think of what it would take to be able to go through to the other end? Think about the issues you have to surmount to be able to pass well in a pending exam; or the obstacles you have to face rising to the top position in your company. Think of the procedures you have to go through to marry the woman you love, or to get that good job you are seeking, or to get that scholarship to pursue further studies. All these look like driving through a dense forest.

Ask yourself this question: Is it the strength of the obstacles that matters or what it takes to go through the obstacles? How are you preparing yourself to go through the troop confronting you each time you open your eyes from sleep? Can you get help from today's memory verse?

Making it Personal

What one specific truth is God teaching me tod ay? ....
....
....
....

One way to practically apply what God has taught me today ....
....
....
....

What do I want to tell God today concerning what He taught me? [***My Prayer***] ....
....
....
....

My Personal Declaration for Today [***Write it down and speak it over and over***] ....
....
....
....

SHAKE OFF THE DUST

Meditate on Hebrews 12:1-4

Memorize 2 Timothy 2:3-4

Thou therefore endure hardness, as a good soldier of Jesus Christ. No man that warreth entangleth himself with the affairs of this life; that he may please him who hath chosen him to be a soldier.

Make it Real

Sometimes one wonders why athletes dress the way they do. Never in the history of athletics has there been a male athlete dressed in a shirt and tie with shoes on his feet or a female athlete dressed in a frock with high hills. The reason is obvious. Those clothes will be inappropriate for competing in a race.

This is not just a natural principle for athletes. It is a spiritual principle for the Christian life. No wonder the Apostle Paul likens the Christian life to a race. He talks about running according to the rules; but beyond the rules, no one forces the runner to use inappropriate clothes that will impede his/her progress in the events.

It is in the light of this truth the Apostle urges us to lay aside every weight. Normally sins are obvious and every Christian tries to run away from situations that have the appearance of sin so they will not be tempted to sin. Weights usually may not initially look like tempting situations. They may seem harmless, yet are dangerous and often takes the Christian unawares.

For example, a married Christian male who still maintains friendship with his former girl friend and maintains nothing is going on between them. That easily constitutes a weight he may have to lay aside. Think through as many issues that sincerely qualify as weights in your life and decide how you are going to gradually shed them off.

Making it Personal

What one specific truth is God teaching me tod ay?..
....
....
....

One way to practically apply what God has taught me today...
....
....
....

What do I want to tell God today concerning what He taught me? [*My Prayer*]....................................
....
....
....

My Personal Declaration for Today [*Write it down and speak it over and over*]...........................
....
....
....

RISE SEVEN TIMES

Meditate on Micah 7:7-10

Memorize Proverbs 24:15-16

Lay not wait, O wicked man, against the dwelling of the righteous; spoil not his resting place: For a just man falleth seven times, and riseth up again: but the wicked shall fall into mischief.

Make it Real

Imagine this scenario of a boxing fight with a lot of money to win. There was a much awaited fight between two famous boxes. Most people thought the fight was a mismatch because one boxer who was slightly taller, stouter and more heavily built was pitched against a less stocky opponent slightly lower in weight than his opponent. In the earlier rounds, the second opponent took heavy blows from the stockier boxer. He fell a couple of times and got up the first time at the count of seven. The second time he fell, he got up at the count of nine. The fight continued until somehow in the three rounds left for the fight to be over, this boxer who had been down twice threw a powerful left hook that sent the opponent down. He could not make the count of ten and the fight was over. Everyone was shocked but had to live with that reality.

The Christian life is like fighting in a boxing ring. Sometimes, one fights aimlessly and becomes vulnerable to attacks from the enemy. A number of times, one may give in to a temptation and fall. There have been reported experiences of people who often were down with one temptation or the other and still got up to continue. As a Christian, it is not how often you fall but how quickly you rise up to continue fighting.

To say that difficulties will not come your way is a lie. To say that you will experience victory in all situations all the time is a possibility but sometimes that does not happen. Going through today's scriptures, identify ways in which a Christian can arm himself so he can minimize falling and also rise up as many times as he falls.

Making it Personal

What one specific truth is God teaching me today?

....

....

....

....

One way to practically apply what God has taught me today...

....

....

....

What do I want to tell God today concerning what He taught me? [**My Prayer**]...

....

....

....

My Personal Declaration for Today [**Write it down and speak it over and over**].................................

....

....

....

NO RETREAT, NO SURRENDER

Meditate on Luke 8:22-25

Memorize Romans 8:18

For I reckon that the sufferings of this present time are not worthy to be compared with the glory which shall be revealed in us.

Make it Real

A man set out to visit his mother in law who was on her death bed and had asked him to come immediately. Her intent was to hand over some family treasure to him for custody till her granddaughter reached the age of accountability. The first vehicle he boarded developed a problem with its engine about a third of the journey and they all had to board another vehicle. This second vehicle traveled about half of the distance left to reach the destination and developed an electrical fault and could not continue the journey.

By this time it was getting dark. They felt if they were able to walk about half of the distance left from where this latest incident happened, there was the possibility of getting a vehicle to complete their journey. Some of the people declined and discontinued the journey since it was easier getting vehicles going in the opposite direction. One particular man was tempted to join the others who crossed to the other side of the road to board vehicles going back. Suddenly, he remembered a phrase he had heard before, "no surrender, no retreat".

Then, our passage for today came back to him. He remembered that when Jesus said, "let us go to the other side, they eventually got there. He thought about the treasure and started walking to the next town as had been suggested earlier.

Meditate on our passage and memory verse again. The man in our journey was going to receive a treasure that he could not take beyond the grave. Can you compare that with a treasure God has prepared for us beyond our current life on earth? How often have you been faced with the decision to call it quits as a Christian? What kept you going?

Making it Personal

What one specific truth is God teaching me today?

....

....

....

....

One way to practically apply what God has taught me today..

....

....

....

What do I want to tell God today concerning what He taught me? [**My Prayer**].......................................

....

....

....

My Personal Declaration for Today [**Write it down and speak it over and over**] ....

....

....

....

....

FAILURE A STEPPING STONE

Meditate on 2 Corinthians 12:1-10

Memorize 2 Corinthians 12:9

And he said unto me, My grace is sufficient for thee: for my strength is made perfect in weakness. Most gladly therefore will I rather glory in my infirmities, that the power of Christ may rest upon me.

Make it Real

Bridges have become a normal thing in the world today. Whoever thought of bridges and started designing bridges was definitely thinking according to God's will and purpose. Without bridges, travelers cannot travel across to towns separated by a river. With bridges, we have dominated waterways that separated one people from another

Today, I want us to look at a peculiar bridge. You can call it a mental bridge because it resides in the mind. It does not take physical bulldozers to remove it. It is called failure. It is difficult for the normal human mind to think of failure as a bridge.

Can you remember a time in your life you studied hard for an exam and you were sure you were going to pass and when the results came you had failed? Can you think of a very close friend or a relative who started a business very well and not so long it all collapsed and he went bankrupt? Those are moments of pain and possible frustration.

Failure usually reflects our weaknesses. That is what potentially creates the problem in our mind. Beyond the apparent hurt and disappointment, failure says "do not go that way again". God says all things work together for good to those who love Him; and that is the verse that takes away the knock-out punch from failure and gives it that positive identity.

Mediate on today's memory verse again and think of the Apostle Paul's take on personal weaknesses. Do they present failure as a bridge?

Making it Personal

What one specific truth is God teaching me today?

....

....

....

....

One way to practically apply what God has taught me today...

....

....

....

*What do I want to tell God today concerning what He taught me? [**My Prayer**]*......................................

....

....

....

*My Personal Declaration for Today [**Write it down and speak it over and over**]*.................................

....

....

....

COUNTING YOUR BLESSINGS

Take this opportunity to reflect over what you have learned in your interaction with God this week. It will be helpful if you write down your experiences

1. Of the lessons or truths God taught you this week, write down which one ministered to you above all the others?

   ....

   ....

   ....

2. Mention one experience you had this week that made that particular lesson or truth more real to you than before?...

   ....

   ....

   ....

3. What was the verse that you were able to memorize out of the verses presented for the week?..

....
....
....

4. Reflect over the lessons for the week. Pray and make the following Prophetic Declarations for the coming week

By divine authority I declare that no obstacle will prevent me from entering my divine destiny in the name of Jesus.

I shake off every weight and break all demonic snares; let the shackles be broken and let all chains fall now in the name of Jesus.

I refuse to retreat in the face of opposition; let the nay sayers be confounded and let their predications be aborted in the name of Jesus.

I pull down demonic towers erected to block my way - let the foundations of the wicked be destroyed and let their wickedness come to an end in the name of Jesus.

Let all contentions cease, and let every obstacle put in my way become a stepping stone to my breakthrough in the name of Jesus.

FORGET THE PAST

Meditate on Isaiah 43:15-19

Memorize Philippians 3:13-14

Forgetting those things which are behind and reaching forward to those things which are ahead, I press toward the goal for the prize of the upward call of God in Christ Jesus.

Make it Real

God gave us a very important organ located in our head called the brain. Naturally, the brain is the center of all human activities. One of the critical functions of the brain is its ability to store information fed to it for several years. As you read the next word, you can pause and send your mind back to those kindergarten years and recall your teachers and how they related with you, etc. That is the power of memory.

Since Man fell in the Garden, everything about us changed, including the experiences God intended us to have on earth. The new reality we live with is that God does not want us to remember many things. In this new reality, God asks us to forget the past. There are things in the past that did not go the way God wanted them to go. Constantly thinking and meditating on them does not help us. In fact it pulls us back.

It is interesting how God asks us to forget even the good things we experienced in the past. God does not mean we should wipe off any good experiences we had with Him; those good experiences form the basis of true praise and worship. Read the passage today and see if you can get the reason for that statement.

If you always live in the past, you lack the power to look into the future to see all the possibilities God has placed there for you. A great man of God who is gone to glory often made the statement, "the best is yet to come" Can you see how that can help understand the passage for today?

Making it Personal

What one specific truth is God teaching me today?

....

....

....

....

One way to practically apply what God has taught me today..

....

....

....

What do I want to tell God today concerning what He taught me? [**My Prayer**]..

....

....

....

My Personal Declaration for Today [**Write it down and speak it over and over**] ....

....

....

....

....

HOW HIGH IS YOUR STANDARD?

Meditate on Exodus 28:1-5

> **Memorize** Philippians 4:8
>
> *Finally, brothers, whatever is true, whatever is honorable, whatever is just, whatever is pure, whatever is lovely, whatever is commendable, if there is any excellence, if there is anything worthy of praise, think about these things.*

Make it Real

In athletic competitions one of the field events that I find interesting is the high jump. In this event, the contestants are started on a certain level that is relatively easy for most of them to jump without faltering. Subsequently, the level is raised higher and higher till several of the athletes are eliminated. The goal of the organizers is to get the best three contestants by raising the bar. You cannot keep the bar low and get the best; everyone will jump that.

In thinking about standards, today's passage provides a guide. Note how detailed God was in His instructions concerning the creation of Aaron's robe. God does not want anything sub-standard. He does not believe in mediocrity; and He has not lowered the bar for us.

Several times, Jesus made the statement, "you have heard of old" Each time Jesus used those introductory statements, you can be sure He was about to raise the standard. Compare killing with being angry without a cause, or adultery with lusting in your heart; then you can truly see what raising the bar means.

Can you hear God saying to you that He is standing by your side and He is ready to provide all you need for as high and as far as you want to go serving in his vineyard and laying for yourself treasures in heaven? Reflect on the goals you set for yourself at the beginning of the year. How high are the targets you set for yourself?

Making it Personal

What one specific truth is God teaching me today?

....

....

....

....

One way to practically apply what God has taught me today...

....

....

....

*What do I want to tell God today concerning what He taught me? [**My Prayer**]*...

....

....

....

*My Personal Declaration for Today [**Write it down and speak it over and over**]*...

....

....

....

HOPE BEYOND THE HOPELESS

Meditate on Genesis 21:1-6

> **Memorize** Matthew 19:26
>
> *But Jesus beheld them, and said unto them, with men this is impossible; but with God all things are possible.*

Make it Real

When a woman grows past the age of 35 and she is not married, one thing becomes of great concern to her – bearing children. One often hears women talking about their biological clock ticking; that is to signify they are becoming concerned about child-bearing. God worked beyond what is usually considered natural; when in their old age, Abraham and Sarah had a child – the child of promise.

This event can easily be referred to as "hope beyond the hopeless". Sarah's example and a number of testimonies in our time, of women who had children after the age of fifty introduce hope in seemingly hopeless situations.

Let us take this natural occurrence into other areas of our lives on earth. Very often we encounter disappointments in situations to the point that we give up hope – after failing an exam three times, after applying for a job with several organizations with no response; after being denied visa to travel abroad several times; when you have invested in a business and no profit seems to be in sight? The natural tendency is to give up.

The call to hope against the hopeless is rooted in the God who makes all things new; the God to whom nothing is impossible, the God who holds all things by the word of His power. If it were not for Him, the call to hope against the hopeless would not hold for any situations. If Lazarus died, was buried for days and God raised him from the dead, what situations are you facing in your life that you have labeled, "hopeless"?

Making it Personal

What one specific truth is God teaching me today?

....

....

....

....

One way to practically apply what God has taught me today..

....

....

....

What do I want to tell God today concerning what He taught me? [**My Prayer**]..

....

....

....

My Personal Declaration for Today [**Write it down and speak it over and over**] ....

....

....

....

....

LET FAITH RISE ABOVE FEAR

Meditate on 1 Samuel 17:1-11; 32-37

> **Memorize** 2 Timothy 1:7
>
> *For God hath not given us the spirit of fear; but of power, and of love, and of a sound mind.*

Make it Real

Take time to read over the passage for today. You may be familiar with this story but take time to meditate on it again. Identify the principal players in the story. Try and evaluate the emotional state of all the parties mentioned here – first Goliath, and then the entire host of Israel. Goliath seemed to be having a field day. He denounced the armies of Israel with his words day after day. Note the emotional state of the leadership and the entire armies of Israel – they were dismayed and terrified. Fear had gripped them right to the core. There was no life and no hope in the children of Israel as they heard the threats of Goliath.

Today, the child of God may be confronted not with a man with the physical stature of Goliath, but confronted with life situations that may be more threatening than Goliath. It may be a pending exam you have to take that will determine if you will be promoted in your workplace; an interview you are going to attend in a couple of weeks that determines whether you will get the job you so much love; or the justification you have to prove to a committee that would enable you win that 300 million dollar contract. Whatever it may be in your case, the situation in the natural creates fear, anxiety and panic, and destabilizes you emotionally. You are afraid of the outcomes.

That is the moment when you need to do what David did in the passages above.

David's attitude is what the Apostle Paul wrote about to Timothy in our memory verse. Can you say that to yourself as you prepare to face that seemingly terrifying situation you are faced with?

Making it Personal

What one specific truth is God teaching me today?

....
....
....
....

One way to practically apply what God has taught me today...

....
....
....

*What do I want to tell God today concerning what He taught me? [**My Prayer**]*...

....
....
....

*My Personal Declaration for Today [**Write it down and speak it over and over**]*......................................

....
....
....

MARCHING ON

Meditate on Joshua 2:1-12

Memorize Matthew 16:18

I will build my Church and the gates of hell shall not prevail against it.

Make it Real

Can you imagine if news comes to the house of government, in our case the Presidential Palace that an army from North Africa is advancing towards our country Ghana and they are almost close to Burkina Faso, which is directly north to our country? What will the President do? A wise President will do a quick reconnaissance to determine the strength of the advancing army. If he is convinced that we are able to combat whatever force they are coming with, there will be no panic in this country. If not, one can imagine the chaos that will prevail here in our country!

Such was the situation described in our passage for today. A powerful army was advancing towards the city of Jericho. Read through the passage again to get the description Rahab gave of that army hence her reason for hiding the two spies.

The army that was advancing in the name of the Lord was definitely not a weak army and Rahab did not mince words about that. It was an army that created fear in its enemies with its presence. It was an army before whom no man could stand and prevail. Above all, it was an army whose power was not from the arm of flesh.

That is the nature of the army you were enrolled in from the day you gave your life to Christ as Saviour and Lord. Can you imagine what it will be like if the church takes up the task of evangelism more seriously than we have over the past three or four decades, and decide that the kingdoms of this world should become the kingdoms of our Lord and Christ? That is where Jesus' declaration in today's memory verse comes alive. Jesus certainly never envisaged a sleeping church when He made that declaration. What is keeping the church from advancing to take the world for Jesus?

Making it Personal

What one specific truth is God teaching me tod ay? ....
....
....
....

One way to practically apply what God has taught me today ....
....
....
....

What do I want to tell God today concerning what He taught me? [**My Prayer**] ....
....
....
....

My Personal Declaration for Today [**Write it down and speak it over and over**] ....
....
....
....

COMBATTING OBSTACLES

Meditate on Daniel 10:1-12

Memorize Matthew 17:20

And Jesus said unto them, Because of your unbelief: for verily I say unto you, If ye have faith as a grain of mustard seed, ye shall say unto this mountain, Remove hence to yonder place; and it shall remove; and nothing shall be impossible unto you.

Make it Real

In a typical steeple chase event in an athletic competition, obstacles are intentionally placed on the track for athletes to encounter and overcome. These are like the hurdles of a 110 meters race. The athletes are expected to run and also jump over the hurdles. The athlete who effectively jumps over these as he also runs as fast as he can wins the race.

Life is full of obstacles. An obstacle refers to something that interferes with or prevents action or progress. It is something, material or nonmaterial, that stands in the way of literal or figurative progress. Day after day as we pursue the issues of this life, we encounter several categories of obstacles which we have to overcome if we must make progress in our lives. Obstacles have become a part of our daily experiences.

In our passage for today, Daniel encountered an obstacle he was not even aware of. From the passage we can learn how Daniel combated this obstacle. The problem we often have is that when we encounter obstacles that we can see with our eyes or we can clearly perceive in our minds, we tend to use the wrong means to combat these obstacles.

From Daniel's experience, we can learn the one inevitable way of overcoming obstacles. That was what Daniel's method of combating the impediment to the point that the answer to his prayer eventually came. Read and meditate on today's passage again, and try to figure out Daniel's method of dealing with obstacles and build your life around it.

Making it Personal

What one specific truth is God teaching me tod ay?..

....

....

....

One way to practically apply what God has taught me today..

....

....

....

What do I want to tell God today concerning what He taught me? [**My Prayer**]..

....

....

....

My Personal Declaration for Today [**Write it down and speak it over and over**] ....

....

....

....

....

COUNTING YOUR BLESSINGS

Take this opportunity to reflect over what you have learned in your interaction with God this week. It will be helpful if you write down your experiences

1. Of the lessons or truths God taught you this week, write down which one ministered to you above all the others?

   ....
   ....
   ....
   ....

2. Mention one experience you had this week that made that particular lesson or truth more real to you than before? ....

   ....
   ....
   ....
   ....

3. What was the verse that you were able to memorize out of the verses presented for the week? ....

....

....

....

4. Reflect over the lessons for the week. Pray and make the following Prophetic Declarations for the coming week

I declare in the name of Jesus, that in spite of all the challenges I have been through, I choose to forget the past and press on.

I match on in the name of Jesus, combating all obstacles on the way to my desired breakthrough.

I lift my faith and I look beyond the hills to the God of my salvation. He will make my feet like hinds feet; he will cause me to walk upon my high places.

I rebuke every spirit of fear, I rebuke every storm in the name of Jesus; I hope in the God of my salvation.

The Lord is my strength and my song; He has become my salvation. Amen

SELF-RESPECT

Meditate on 1 Samuel 16:1-12

Memorize 1Timothy 4:12

Let no man despise thy youth; but be thou an example of the believers, in word, in conversation, in charity, in spirit, in faith, in purity.

Make it Real

Our passage today reminds us of one of the realities of human life. The Prophet had been asked by God to anoint a new king for Israel following the disobedience and subsequent rejection of Saul as King. As the story goes, the prophet of God used what he thought was a good criteria for deciding whom God had chosen. God corrected him and gave him His own criteria.

In as much as God's principle overshadowed Samuel's, the story nonetheless underscores what usually occurs in human relationships. We give honor and respect to people based on certain observations we make of them. If you flip it over, we can say that we give respect to people based on how they present themselves to us. It is appropriate to say that people respect you based on how you present yourself to them.

That brings us to our memory verse for today. The Apostle Paul in exhorting Timothy strongly implied that Timothy was responsible for how people responded to his leadership. Paul believed that it was Timothy who could allow people to despise him. In other words, self-respect is what will make others respect you too. He told Timothy what to do in order to earn the respect of all under his leadership.

This principle runs through families, corporate organizations, clubs and in practically every gathering where people interact on a regular basis. Self-respect remains one major basis for earning the respect of others. Ponder over what you have done in the past couple of weeks that promoted or robbed you of earning the respect of the people around you.

Making it Personal

What one specific truth is God teaching me today?

....

....

....

....

One way to practically apply what God has taught me today..

....

....

....

What do I want to tell God today concerning what He taught me? [**My Prayer**]...................................

....

....

....

My Personal Declaration for Today [**Write it down and speak it over and over**] ....

....

....

....

....

NOT TOSSED TO AND FRO

Meditate on Ephesians 4:10-16

> **Memorize** Colossians 2:6-7
>
> *As ye have therefore received Christ Jesus the Lord, so walk ye in him: Rooted and built up in him, and stablished in the faith, as ye have been taught, abounding therein with thanksgiving.*

Make it Real

In a drawing competition, contestants were asked to paint a picture symbolizing peace. The three topmost paintings included first, a man sitting in a room with nothing in the room except the chair he sat on, with his chin in the palms of his hands. The second painting was a man sitting in a canoe out there in a sea that was very calm and serene. The third painting was a bird perching on a tree whose branches were being blown vigorously by the wind whilst the bird still quietly perched on the branch. The third painting won the award. When asked why, the organizers argued that peace is not when all around you is calm but peace is when all around you seems very rough yet you remain calm in the midst of the situation; that was the case with the bird. The winds did not get the bird jumping from tree to tree. It just continued to stay on its perch.

Our passage today alerts us to the reality that there are going to be several doctrines parading around the world. Paul mentioned that when he spoke about doctrines of devils in the last days. We are already living in those times when every month one hears some strange and outrageous teaching that is supposed to be Christian.

The Apostle Paul does not leave us with just a warning. He also tells us how we can be strong and prevent being tossed to and fro by these doctrines. He teaches us what to do no matter how violent the winds of false doctrine blow in our world.

Making it Personal

What one specific truth is God teaching me tod ay?..
....
....
....

One way to practically apply what God has taught me today...
....
....
....

*What do I want to tell God today concerning what He taught me? [**My Prayer**]*...
....
....
....

*My Personal Declaration for Today [**Write it down and speak it over and over**]* ....
....
....
....
....

RESPECT OTHERS

Meditate on Luke 13:10-17

> **Memorize** Romans 12:10
>
> *Be kindly affectioned one to another with brotherly love; in honour preferring one another;*

Make it Real

One area where most people fall short in their relationships is respecting others. As humans, our criteria for respecting others are often far removed from God's standards. We tend to respect people for basically three reasons: money, physical looks and fame. It is not uncommon to find people literally bowing at the feet of others because they have or display a show of wealth. We do the same for the people who have become famous for several reasons – achievement in sports, music, etc. The sad truth is that people who do not fall in any of these categories mentioned above seem to get little or no respect at all from the rest of society.

Jesus demonstrated profoundly the reason we should respect people. Can you glean that from the passage by Jesus' statement before healing the woman? She is the daughter of Abraham. In other words, she is of value to God. It is her value before God that earned her healing on the Sabbath day; not what she looked like on the outside.

Every day, we pass by several people who do not look like they deserve our respect. Jesus expects us to acknowledge people not for the great things they have accomplished in this life, but for who they are – made in the image of God, redeemed by the precious blood of the Lamb and citizens of our heavenly kingdom. Remember this extends even to those who are yet to believe in Jesus.

How did you treat the taxi driver who picked you this morning for work, or the driver's mate or Bus Conductor who took the transport fare on the vehicle you boarded to office, or the security man at the entrance of your office, or the house help who takes care of your home?

Making it Personal

What one specific truth is God teaching me today?

....
....
....
....

One way to practically apply what God has taught me today..

....
....
....

What do I want to tell God today concerning what He taught me? **[My Prayer]**..

....
....
....

My Personal Declaration for Today **[Write it down and speak it over and over]** ....

....
....
....
....

WALK IN DISCIPLINE

Meditate on 1 Corinthians 9:24-27

Memorize Galatians 5:24-25

And they that are Christ's have crucified the flesh with the affections and lusts. If we live in the Spirit, let us also walk in the Spirit.

Make it Real

Discipline is one word that is fast being pushed in the background in the church today. Somehow the idea of discipline only sends them back to those primary school years where one had a very strict teacher who insisted that everyone obeyed the school rules and regulations or got punished. Some have also spoken of fathers who were so strict and uncompromising that they ended up having no fellowship with their children because they were afraid of them. These and other images put discipline in a wrong perspective.

The Apostle Paul makes us understand that discipline is not necessarily something happening from the external. Waiting for someone to "discipline" us is what gets us into all kinds of problems; because the truth is that discipline is more situated within the individual than from without. Every man has the singular opportunity to draw from the grace of God to keep his flesh under control, and that is what constitutes discipline.

We hear statements like absolute power corrupts absolutely. That simply is someone's inability to control his flesh. Talk about a man who is living an adulterous life not with one woman, but many; that also shows lack of control of the flesh. If an accountant continuously forges documents and falsifies figures so he can get more money, that is another example of lack of control of the flesh and that also is indiscipline. Young people talk of peer pressure and blame their behavior on their peers. The truth is that their peers did not make them fall into sin. It is an issue of lack of self-control.

Ponder a bit on what lessons we can learn from the Apostle Paul in this regard.

Making it Personal

What one specific truth is God teaching me today?

....

....

....

....

One way to practically apply what God has taught me today..

....

....

....

*What do I want to tell God today concerning what He taught me? [**My Prayer**]*..

....

....

....

*My Personal Declaration for Today [**Write it down and speak it over and over**]* ....

....

....

....

....

BE A VESSEL OF HONOR

Meditate on 2 Timothy 2:19-22

Memorize Romans 6:12-13

Let not sin therefore reign in your mortal body, that ye should obey it in the lusts thereof. Neither yield ye your members as instruments of unrighteousness unto sin: but yield yourselves unto God, as those that are alive from the dead, and your members as instruments of righteousness unto God.

Make it Real

No one ever thought that wicked men would fly an airplane into a building like it happened in the United States in the year 2001. The reason is simple; the airplane is not an instrument for killing people. It is meant to convey people from one place to another. Think also of the many instruments we use in our homes. The one who designed the knife did not make it as a weapon for murder. It was meant to cut things up in the kitchen to make cooking easier. Similarly, other instruments have been misused like the above mentioned ones.

The Apostle Paul is talking here about our human bodies and all the parts thereof as instruments. We can glean from the passages that one can either be an instrument in God's hands or make oneself an instrument in the hands of the devil.

For us who have had the privilege of knowing Jesus as Lord and Savior, the Apostle Paul implores us to yield ourselves unto God. In the instruction to Timothy he explains what purging ourselves of all filthiness makes us become in God's hands – vessels of honor.

Although no man can actually tell God what He should exactly use him for, one is certain that making yourself available to God by purging yourself from all unclean things definitely makes you available to God for noble use.

How are you fulfilling your portion of this deal? Take time to identify what things in your life constitute filth that needs to be purged. Be assured that the Holy Spirit is with you to help you get rid of anything you see as filth in your life.

Making it Personal

What one specific truth is God teaching me today?

....

....

....

....

One way to practically apply what God has taught me today..

....

....

....

*What do I want to tell God today concerning what He taught me? [**My Prayer**]*..

....

....

....

*My Personal Declaration for Today [**Write it down and speak it over and over**]* ....

....

....

....

....

KEEPING YOUR LIGHT BURNING

Meditate on 1 Peter 2:6-12

> **Memorize** Ephesians 5:8
>
> *For ye were sometimes darkness, but now are ye light in the Lord: walk as children of light*

Make it Real

Have you noticed that when the high lights of a car are put on when it is not dark, the effect of the lights is not felt as much as when it is dark? That is an astute observation. The power of light is manifested best not in light but in darkness. The world seems to be getting darker and darker by the day. With the passing of every day, news from around the world set everyone on edge, not knowing what next is going to happen.

Among those things happening is the myriad of philosophies and ideologies that often confront the fundamental beliefs of the Christian faith, including the values God expects us to live by. Alternate lifestyles and ways of doing things continue to flood the corridors of life to the point that the Christian sometimes is at a loss regarding what is right and what is wrong. That is what our world has come to and we have to confront that reality.

In the midst of all these, it is appropriate to say that as children of God, this is time for our light to burn even brighter. In a world of darkness, our Christian testimony is expected to stand out as both example and hope for many who are giving up on life.

The most powerful tool the Christian has to confront the darkness of this world is not wealth. Even if God blesses the church and it becomes financially very wealthy, that is not what will get the world's attention. What will get the world's attention today is the life of Christ manifested by every Christian everywhere on this planet. The world will marvel at the effect of our Christian witness in a dark world. This is the time for our light to burn even brighter than before. How bright is your light?

Making it Personal

What one specific truth is God teaching me today?

....

....

....

....

One way to practically apply what God has taught me today...

....

....

....

*What do I want to tell God today concerning what He taught me? [**My Prayer**]*..

....

....

....

*My Personal Declaration for Today [**Write it down and speak it over and over**]* ....

....

....

....

....

COUNTING YOUR BLESSINGS

> *Take this opportunity to reflect over what you have learned in your interaction with God this week. It will be helpful if you write down your experiences*

1. Of the lessons or truths God taught you this week, write down which one ministered to you above all the others?

   ....
   ....
   ....

2. Mention one experience you had this week that made that particular lesson or truth more real to you than before?

   ....
   ....
   ....

3. What was the verse that you were able to memorize out of the verses presented for the week? ....

....

....

....

4. Reflect over the lessons for the week. Pray and make the following Prophetic Declarations for the coming week

I declare in the name of Jesus, that as I stay in the word, I will not be tossed to and fro by every wind of doctrine.

My leadership will not be despised; I will be an example to the believers and unbelievers alike by my word and conduct by the grace of God.

I will treat others with respect and dignity; I will not be a disrespectful and an undisciplined believer in the name of Jesus.

As I continue to purge myself by the word, I will be a vessel of honor fit for the

Master's use in the name of Jesus.

By the grace of God and through the power of the word in my heart, I declare that I will continue to be a shining light in a dark and perverse world; the Lord being my helper. Amen

GOD HAS YOUR NEEDS COVERED

Meditate on Matthew 6:25-34

Memorize Psalm 37:4-5

Delight thyself also in the LORD: and he shall give thee the desires of thine heart.

Commit thy way unto the LORD; trust also in him; and he shall bring it to pass.

Make it Real

The average human being is seriously concerned about his life on earth. As a matter of fact not many people live in this life with eternity in mind. People live by what they see, what they hear and by extension, what they can get in this life. A lot of life's activities currently are geared more towards our earthly existence than about eternity. Very often our needs on earth overwhelm us and make eternity look so remote we do not want to even think about the reality of life after death.

261

Such a state of affairs is quite understandable. We live in the physical and do a lot of spiritual things even in the physical. The only problem with living exclusively- being influenced by physical needs is that it often competes with issues of faith and dependence on God. We think we have to make sure that we have all we need for this life to the point we forget that God knows our needs more than we want to believe.

Can you pause and think that it is only after God had created all that man would need for his existence on earth that He finally created Man? From the early days of the earth, God has demonstrated His concern for the welfare of the man He put on earth. It is unlikely that the resources of the earth will be depleted. We have not discovered even half of what God deposited in the earth before He created man.

If we remember that God is the Source of all that we pursue in this life, we will definitely make Him a part of everything we do, including the pursuit of what we need to live our lives on earth.

Making it Personal

What one specific truth is God teaching me today?

....

....

....

....

One way to practically apply what God has taught me today..

....

....

....

What do I want to tell God today concerning what He taught me? [**My Prayer**]..

....

....

....

My Personal Declaration for Today [**Write it down and speak it over and over**]............

....

....

....

....

YOUR INHERITANCE IS INTACT

Meditate on Matthew 19:27-30

Memorize 1 Peter 1:3-4

Blessed be the God and Father of our Lord Jesus Christ, which according to his abundant mercy hath begotten us again unto a lively hope by the resurrection of Jesus Christ from the dead, To an inheritance incorruptible, and undefiled, and that fadeth not away, reserved in heaven for you

---

Make it Real

Today's passage is a conversation the disciples had with Jesus. It centered on what was in store for them, now that they had left everything to follow Jesus. Jesus did not rebuke them for their honesty; He took the opportunity to instruct them on one reality about the life He had called them to. No one follows Jesus and becomes worse off. The gains are numerous and they transcend even life on earth.

The Christian life is a call to be heavenly-minded. Sometimes people misinterpret this to make it look like if you are heavenly-minded, you may lose all that pertain to life on earth here. Ponder over the conversation that went on between Jesus and His disciples in our passage for today, as also emphasized by our memory verse.

Jesus re-affirmed that the believer's inheritance in Christ is intact. No man can touch it. He even goes on to assure them that their inheritance in Christ is not limited to what anyone thinks he is sacrificing to follow Jesus. Whatever you have left to follow Jesus, you gain several fold in this life, and Jesus adds what you did not think of – a life of eternal joy and peace with Him when all life here on earth is over. Nothing can beat that!

Making it Personal

What one specific truth is God teaching me today?

....

....

....

....

One way to practically apply what God has taught me today...

....

....

....

*What do I want to tell God today concerning what He taught me? [**My Prayer**]*...

....

....

....

*My Personal Declaration for Today [**Write it down and speak it over and over**]*..

....

....

....

TAKING YOUR POSSESSIONS BY PRAYER

Meditate on Philippians 4:4-7

Memorize Mathew 11:12

And from the days of John the Baptist until now the kingdom of heaven suffereth violence, and the violent take it by force.

Make it Real

The believer's inheritance is twofold – first, the numerous material and earthly blessings that God promised all who come to Christ. God' intention is not that you live a miserable life on earth because He has a life in heaven for you. His plan is that you enjoy the life He has for you here on earth, and then, to continue to enjoy even more when you come over to live with Him after death forever and ever.

Your inheritance in heaven is intact and no one can touch it. The inheritance that is earthly however often becomes subjected to the elements of the earth, including activities of the devil and his cohorts, trying to rob you of your due on earth. That introduces the need for spiritual warfare to possess your possessions.

It is not a physical fight where you go about quarrelling with everyone around you. It is not a fight of the flesh where you resort to all human tactics, sometimes by foul means because you must possess your possessions here on earth by all means. It is a spiritual fight and that simply means you involve God the Father, God the Son and God the Holy Spirit in that fight. That is where a lot of people miss it. They think it is their fight and in the process they end up losing because they fight not according to the rules God has instituted for spiritual warfare.

You have the privilege of employing all the types of prayers available in the scriptures to possess your possessions. When the battle is won in the spirit, the natural issues just give way. God is certainly waiting on you to get Him through His word to fight on your behalf.

Making it Personal

What one specific truth is God teaching me today?

....

....

....

....

One way to practically apply what God has taught me today...

....

....

....

What do I want to tell God today concerning what He taught me? [**My Prayer**] ....

....

....

....

My Personal Declaration for Today [**Write it down and speak it over and over**] ....

....

....

....

....

HONOR THE GIVER

Meditate on Deuteronomy 8:10-19

> **Memorize** Proverbs 3:9-10
>
> *Honour the LORD with thy substance, and with the first fruits of all thine increase:*
>
> *So shall thy barns be filled with plenty, and thy presses shall burst out with new wine.*

Make it Real

It is easy to know if a man honors God by his attitude to whatever material and other blessings he is enjoying in this life. It is easy to find people who believe that it is by their sweat and toil they have earned whatever they have.

Let us get it clear – God acknowledges for example, that as a medical doctor you burned the midnight oil – studying and spent all the time needed in the laboratory and in the hospital. As a business man He acknowledges the travels you made, those decisions you took that no one understood but you took anyway. God acknowledges every effort you put in to obtain your inheritance. Nevertheless, He wants you to know that your efforts would have amounted to nothing if He had not favored you. The truth about this principle of God's favor is that it does not apply only to the Christian. It applies to the unbeliever who is doing clean, genuine business – not the cocaine pushers and the gamblers.

All God expects of you is that when you have received your inheritance, you duly and fully acknowledge Him. The sin of the world is that the unbelievers boast in their strength and ingenuity, forgetting that no increase comes to any man without the express permission of God. The child of God therefore must not make the same mistake the unbeliever does. You must honor the Giver.

If you truly want to honor God with your blessings, the Holy Spirit will definitely lead you to do things not to please and obtain the praise of men, but to do things that will truly honor God, the Source of your blessings.

Making it Personal

What one specific truth is God teaching me today?

....
....
....
....

One way to practically apply what God has taught me today...
....
....
....

*What do I want to tell God today concerning what He taught me? [**My Prayer**]*...
....
....
....

*My Personal Declaration for Today [**Write it down and speak it over and over**]* ....
....
....
....
....

ACTION CHAPEL PRAYER CATHEDRAL

SERVICE TIMES

SPINTEX ROAD, ACCRA

SUNDAY MORNING SERVICES
7 am - 9:30 am
10 am - 12:30 pm

EVENING SERVICE
6 pm - 8:30 pm

WEDNESDAY (MIDWEEK) SERVICE:
6:30 pm - 8: 30 pm

DOMINION HOUR (Thursdays):
9 am - 12 noon.

MORNING GLORY (Saturdays):
7 am - 9:30 am.

FIRM FOUNDATION SUNDAY SERVICES:
7 am - 9:30 am
10 am - 12: 30 pm

RELEVANCE SUNDAY SERVICE:
3 pm – 4:30pm

For Action branches, fellowship,
and other church activities,
please call +233.302.745.000
or visit www.actionchapel.net

FOLLOW ME ON FACEBOOK!
https://www.facebook.com/archbishopduncanwilliams

Made in the USA
Lexington, KY
11 July 2017